TRANSATLANTIC LINERS 1950–1970

WILLIAM H. MILLER

FONTHILL

For Mick Lindsay, a kind & most generous friend,
and keeper of a great marine photo collection

Front cover illustration: Europa and the Ambrose Lightship off New York. From a painting by Stephen Card.

Rear cover illustration: Eastbound on the *Queen Elizabeth*. (Tim Noble collection)

Fonthill Media Language Policy
Fonthill Media publishes in the international English language market. One language edition is published worldwide. As there are minor differences in spelling and presentation, especially with regard to American English and British English, a policy is necessary to define which form of English to use. The Fonthill Policy is to use the form of English native to the author. William H. Miller was born and educated in the United States; therefore American English has been adopted in this publication.

Fonthill Media Limited
Fonthill Media LLC
www.fonthillmedia.com
office@fonthillmedia.com

First published in the United Kingdom
and the United States of America 2019

British Library Cataloguing in Publication Data:
A catalogue record for this book is available from the British Library

ISBN 978-1-78155-693-1

Typeset in Minion Pro 10pt on 13pt
Printed and bound in England

TRANSATLANTIC LINERS

Contents

Foreword

In the 1950s, my father worked in Manhattan, in a midtown office, and he commuted each day on a Hudson River ferry to and from Weehawken. In summer, during the school holidays, he would sometimes invite me to join him, visit his office, have lunch, and then return on my own (while he returned to his office). One of the highlights was riding those heavily wooded ferries. They were steamers with roaring engines and screeching whistles. I would go up to the upper deck and stand in the open air and look over to Luxury Liner Row. The Atlantic liner business was still going strong and so the piers were often crowded with liners. I began to know them all—the *Andrea Doria*, *Independence*, *United States*, *Île de France*, and the Queens, *Mary* and *Elizabeth*. There would also be the likes of the *Olympia*, *Berlin*, and *Gripsholm*. What a collection, what a cast! And they each had a sense of character, history, an individuality.

Eventually, I stopped using the ferry, and then the liners themselves disappeared in the '60s and especially the '70s. But in 2016, I crossed myself on the *Queen Mary 2*. I attended Bill Miller's insightful and nostalgic talks. For me, it was as if the liners had returned. I am therefore happy to write this short message for his latest book on those wonderful ships of yesteryear.

Brian Whitehead
Chicago, Illinois
Fall 2017

Acknowledgments

TYPICAL TO WRITING ANY BOOK, many hands—like the crew of a ship—have been involved in this project. First, my thanks to Fonthill Media, to Alan Sutton and Jay Slater, for taking on this project. Their effort and work are superb. Noted special appreciation to Tony La Forgia, Mick Lindsay, Michael Hadgis, and Tim Noble, and to Brian Whitehead for his evocative foreword.

Further thanks to the late Frank Andrews, Ernest Arroyo, the late Frank Braynard, Philippe Brebant, Stephen Card, Michael Cassar, Tom Cassidy, Luis Miguel Correia, the late Frank Cronican, the late Alex Duncan, late Richard Faber, the late John Gillespie, Dr. Nico Guns, Des Kirkpatrick, Lindsay Johnstone, Norman Knebel, Peter Knego, Anton Logvinenko, James McNamara, Larry Miller, Selim San, John Tabbut-McCarthy, Stephen L. Tacey, Richard Turnwald, and Al Wilhelmi. Companies and organizations that have assisted include Crystal Cruises, Cunard Line, German-Atlantic Line, the Halifax Maritime Museum, Hoboken Historical Museum, Holland-America Line, Moran Towing & Transportation Co., Port Authority of New York & New Jersey, Princess Cruises, Royal Cruise Lines, Steamship Historical Society of America, World Ocean & Cruise Liner Society, and the World Ship Society. Any omissions are deeply regretted.

Introduction

World War II was indeed disruptive, as well as destructive. A total of 50 percent of all Atlantic liners were gone: bombed, torpedoed, burnt out, or not returned by the military. Luxurious pre-war super liners—ships such as the *Bremen*, *Empress of Britain*, *Rex*, *Conte di Savoia*, and *Normandie*—were gone. Only three ships in the super liner class remained: the *Europa*, *Queen Mary*, and *Queen Elizabeth*.

Restoration and renewal defined the most immediate and most pressing orders of the day. Shipping lines were interested in restoring pre-war passenger services. Governments were anxious as well—reviving trade, delivering the first waves of tourists, and bringing in much-needed American dollars; meanwhile, lots of Europeans, including refugees and displaced persons, sought new lives and new homes overseas.

Getting a berth was not easy in those immediate post-war years. I recall the tales of high-powered, often-rich businessmen having to share doubles and even four-berth rooms in the immediate post-war, in 1946–47, on the likes of the *Queen Mary* and *Queen Elizabeth*. A late lady friend, who was devoted to the French Line and enjoyed the high luxuries of such legendary, pre-war liners such as the *Normandie* and *Île de France*, needed to get to France in 1946. She made do with a berth but in a quad cabin on a French Line freighter, the *Oregon*. Another friend told me of being waitlisted for months for an eastbound crossing to Europe in 1947. While the former German super liner *Europa*, the *USS Europa* after the war, was pressed into westbound service, bringing as many as 9,000 troops home from war-torn Europe, she was all but empty on the return sailings. Without ships, the United States Lines offered a handful of berths to commercial passengers, but it was hardly luxury. On November 30, 1945, for example, the ship departed with sixty passengers aboard. "Passengers will travel comfortably and safely enough to Southampton," said a U.S. Navy spokesman, "But on the way, they will clean their own dishes, put their utensils and mess gear in proper places and make and keep their cabins shipshape. Dining is cafeteria style." A United States Lines' agent added, "We stopped short of asking them to bring along their own carpet sweepers!" There were too few ships—almost 50 percent of the world's pre-war passenger ships were gone by the war's end in the summer of 1945.

Revival! Steam whistles and electric horns hooted and honked. New York harbor was putting out its red carpet—a brand-new ship was arriving. Being just after the dreary, dark days of World War II, it was cause to be happy and hopeful. It was August 1947, and while not a super liner or record-breaking ship, Cunard's 13,300-ton *Media* was arriving in port. Tugs escorted the flag-bedecked ship to her berth along the City's West Side piers. Capped by her sparking orange-red and black funnel, she was, in fact, quite significant: she was the first brand-new passenger ship to be built following the war. She symbolized revival, and more new liners, it was confidently reported, would follow in her wake. Her twin sister, the *Parthia*, as an example, was due in New York for the first time in April 1948.

Of course, new ships were in the works: although small, Sweden's 11,700-ton *Stockholm* had her debut in 1948, while Norway added a new flagship, the *Oslofjord*, a year later. The biggest and possibly most luxurious new post-war liner was Cunard's 34,200-ton *Caronia*. Among her indulgent features, every passenger cabin onboard had private bathroom facilities. In 1951, Holland added the *Ryndam* and *Maasdam*, which offered vastly improved accommodations but in tourist class. John Tabbut-McCarthy and his family often crossed on the 15,000-ton *Ryndam*:

> We loved the little *Ryndam*. She was intimate—and slower and so offered a longer voyage. It was 10 days from, say, Rotterdam to New York with stops at Le Havre, Southampton, sometimes Cobh, and at Halifax two days before New York. She carried a very small first class [thirty-nine berths in all, and 875 in less expensive, less fancy tourist class] and we always occupied the same upper-deck cabins. Mine was done in green. We'd also

Sunrise: The thrill of an early morning arrival at New York. (*Tim Noble collection*)

have the same table in the small, almost private dining room. The table had, as I remember, wooden lips around the edges and was sprinkled with water in rough seas. There was also a little card room, a smoking room and a bar. There was a little staircase up to first class. The ship had a little pool out on deck and we'd go to the tourist class lounge to see movies. I also remember the forward lounge, also in tourist class, which had bamboo chairs and floral-print cushions.

Sorting some of the surviving ships meant uncertainty. Would the giant *Europa*, the pre-war German liner in post-war American hands, be restored for commercial service under the United States Lines house flag? Would she become the new flagship of the American merchant marine? Or would Italy's fire-gutted *Conte di Savoia* be rebuilt for French Line service or for the Holland-America Line? Would the Americans return the likes of the *Saturnia* and *Vulcania* to the Italians or pass them to the Soviets? Would Canadian Pacific construct a big liner to replace the pre-war *Empress of Britain*?

The first half of the 1950s did see something of a grand parade of sorts of new Atlantic liners: ships such as the *Independence & Constitution*, *Flandre*, *Olympia*, *Andrea Doria & Cristoforo Colombo*, *Kungsholm*, and *Bergensfjord*.

In 1950–51, there was some ambitious, and exciting, ideas; however, these never left the drawing board. There was talk that Cunard was thinking of a third Queen, possibly as large as 75,000 tons. The United States Lines was quietly making plans, it was reported, for a 60,000-ton near-sister to the upcoming *United States*. The Swedes were said to be thinking of no less than a pair of 50,000 tonners, their largest liners yet. Yet perhaps most unusual, but least likely, was word that designers in a Leningrad naval shipyard were busily preparing plans for a pair of 50,000 ton, 2,000-berth liners, with simple, less costly accommodation. While there would be lounges and a cinema, the ships would have sparsely decorated cabins and cafeteria-style dining. They would be true to Moscow's proletarian policies and offer Leningrad–New York service.

Unquestionably, the super star of transatlantic travel was the brilliant *United States*, commissioned in the summer of 1952. William Francis Gibbs, America's finest naval architect, had long dreamed of the U.S. having a great super liner of its own. He had made numerous proposals, drawings, and sketches beginning in the 1920s for record-breaking ships flying the red, white, and blue. However, it was not until World War II—especially as the Cunard Queens were ferrying 15,000 troops per crossing at the height of the hostilities—that the U.S. Government released the great importance of a big, fast liner as a military transport. The role as a flag-carrying commercial liner was almost secondary. Gibbs was commissioned to design what would be the most technologically-advanced Atlantic liner of all time. Known as the "the Big Ship" project, his designs began in earnest in 1946. The ship would cost over $70 million, a staggering amount for the time, and would be built at Newport News, Virginia.

Commissioned in the spring of 1952, the *United States* was shielded in U.S. Government secrecy concerning many components, but still fascinated the public. There were 125,000 pieces of chinaware onboard, 4,000 blankets, and her overall design required 1.2 million blueprints. In every way, she was an amazing success, a *tour de force* of post-World War II triumph and distinction. During her trials, for example, it was later revealed that she made 20 knots in reverse, and that she reached a speed of some 43 knots. She was assuredly the fastest, most powerful liner ever, and had an average speed of some 36 knots during her westbound maiden voyage. For the next decade, her success was assured. Everyone, it seemed, wanted to sail aboard the "world's fastest liner." In her first decade of service, the *United States* had an average 98 percent load factor. Only Cunard's Queens were comparable in popularity.

On a June day in 1957, 16,000 European-bound passengers passed through New York's passenger ship piers.

In its September 9, 1957 issue, *Newsweek* magazine heralded the rebirth of Atlantic liner travel. (*Author's collection*)

Business was booming, or so it seemed. A late summer's day that same year saw ten passenger ships arrive: the *Constitution*, *United States*, *Olympia*, *Flandre*, *Mauretania*, *Queen Mary*, *Gripsholm*, *Statendam*, *Maasdam*, and *Exochorda*. The *Britannic* and *Noordam* were already in port, having arrived a day or so before. In the following weeks, the *Queen Elizabeth* arrived from Southampton with some 2,248 passengers, about fifteen more than her posted maximum capacity.

That very same year, airline travel on the Atlantic equaled steamship travel for the first time. The writing was, as has often been said, on the wall. In the following year, in October 1958, the first jets flew between the continents. In a matter of six months, the smiling, aggressive airlines had two-thirds of all trans-ocean clientele and, within five years, 98 percent. Quite simply, the transatlantic liner was doomed.

The great slump: It began with the winter, off-season crossings. Myself, I recall the *Queen Elizabeth* arriving in January 1962 with a scant 175 passengers onboard, the *Carinthia* with ninety and the *Oslofjord* with sixty.

Enthusiasm remained high, optimism in the future very brisk, however. This positivity continued in the late '50s and well into the '60s. The biggest and most extravagant of the new-builds of the late '50s was the *France*, the last of the French "floating palaces." Just as she was under construction and despite the dramatic, very intrusive appearance of the jet, ideas for new passenger ships, including super liners, were still plentiful and optimistic. Along with the likes of the *Rotterdam*, *Leonardo da Vinci*, *Empress of Canada*, and the aforementioned, 66,300-ton *France*, there was actually far more ambitious plans.

Even in the late '50s, there was still lots of interest, projection, enthusiasm, and plans for yet other Atlantic liners. Would the Portuguese build a liner for Lisbon–New York service? Would the Spanish Line go forward with a pair of 20,000-tonners? Would American Export Lines get the go ahead (but with financial help from the U.S. Government) to build a third large liner, dubbed the *Constellation* project? Would Cunard build a three-class liner to replace the aging *Queen Mary*? Would Italy's brand new *Leonardo da Vinci* eventually be refitted with nuclear power? And, most enthusiastic, would several creative businessmen go forward with plans for (super ships)?

In July 1959, New York City-based businessman and hotel owner Hyman B. Cantor signed a contract with a shipyard in Hamburg to study the possible construction of twin 90,000-ton liners for the North Atlantic. These ships, it would seem, would break every record in size and distinction. They would have accommodations for 6,000 passengers and crews of 1,350, and service speeds of 34 knots. It was envisioned that would sail the North Atlantic, between New York, Zeebrugge, and an undetermined port in Germany (but most likely to be Cuxhaven for Hamburg). Catering would be on a cafeteria style and the lowest fare, not including meals, was put at $75. The two ships would cost, it was estimated, $160 million to build. The first of them, to be named *Peace*, would be delivered in August 1962, with the second ship, the *Goodwill*, following in August 1963. Expectedly, the main problem was the financing.

Two months later, in September 1959, businessman Edgar Detwiler had approached a Dutch shipyard for the construction of no less than four even larger passenger liners. Construction of the first was to start with a year, during 1960, and completion expected in 1963. Mr. Detwiler's ships would be 120,000 gross tons and measure 1,275 feet in length and 130 feet in width. They would have a service speed of 35 knots and carry 8,000 passengers with 2,000 crew. They would be slightly less expensive than Mr. Cantor's ships, with fares starting at $65 and including meals. They would sail for the newly-created American-European Lines, fly the Dutch flag, and would be named *United Nations*, *New Yorker*, *Lisbon*, and *Hollander*. The first pair would sail the North Atlantic, between New York, Cobh, Plymouth, and Amsterdam; the second set would run on the mid-Atlantic, between New York, Lisbon, and, on some sailings, to either Naples or Genoa. The ships would use the new, innovative, engines-aft design.

When the mighty *France* steamed into New York harbor for the first time, in February 1962, she was a sensible design: nine months on the Atlantic, three months for winter cruising. But it was all changing, much like the fierce winds of Atlantic storms. Old patterns and formulas, and plans, were swept away. The *Michelangelo* and *Raffaello*, completed in 1965, never earned a single lire; Israel's *Shalom* lasted less than three years before being sold off; the *Sagafjord* turned almost immediately to fulltime cruising; and Home Lines scrapped plans for transatlantic service with the innovative *Oceanic* (instead, she would sail year-round on cruises).

I was among those who watched, in New York's Lower Bay, as the *Queen Elizabeth 2* arrived for the first time, in May 1969. She was big, different, and innovative in ways and said to be the last Atlantic liner. Well, of course, Carnival Corporation, as owners of historic Cunard, changed all that in 2004 when they commissioned the 150,000-ton, 2,600-passenger *Queen Mary 2*, the largest Atlantic liner ever. These days, some of her passengers recall the "good old days," earlier crossings on ships covered in these pages, while others feel nostalgic of having missed it all.

This is a list—from American Banner to Zim Lines—of the last generation of transatlantic passenger ships. I have attempted to be complete, and the range of ships is quite diverse: from the legendary *Queen Mary* to Egypt's little *Star of Assuan*, from the luxurious likes of the *Caronia* to austere student ships such as the *Groote Beer*. I find the ships, all of them, and their careers quite fascinating. It has therefore been a journey, a voyage if you will, to compile this book.

Bill Miller
Secaucus, New Jersey
Winter 2019

Top left: $50 fares to Europe on giant liner was proposed in 1959. (*Author's collection*)

Above left: Excitement was high—the contracts were almost signed. (*Author's collection*)

Above right: Seventy Years. The Evolution of the Liner: *Queen Elizabeth* (1940), *Queen Elizabeth 2* (1969), and *Queen Elizabeth* (2010). (*Cunard*)

1

American Banner Lines

Atlantic (1953)

Service: New York to Zeebrugge and Amsterdam.
Particulars: 14,138 gross tons; 564 × 76 × 28 feet.
Builders: Sun Shipbuilding & Dry Dock Co., Chester, Pennsylvania, 1953.
Machinery: Steam turbines; single screw; service speed 20 knots.
Capacity: Forty first and 860 tourist class.
Notes: Former freighter rebuilt as a passenger ship.

July 1, 1953: Launched as Mariner class freighter *Badger Mariner* for U.S. Maritime Administration, U.S. flag.
October 1953: Entered service.
1957: Sold to American Banner Lines, U.S. flag; renamed *Atlantic*. Rebuilt as a passenger ship by Ingalls Shipbuilding yard, Pascagoula, Mississippi.
June 11, 1958: Entered transatlantic passenger service; unsuccessful.
October 1959: Final American Banner sailing; laid-up at Bethlehem Steel shipyard, Hoboken; later sold to American Export Lines (qv).

Converted from a freighter, American Banner's *Atlantic* arrives in New York harbor for the first time in June 1958. (*Author's collection*)

2

American Export Lines

La Guardia

Service: New York to Naples and Genoa; later extended to Palermo, Piraeus and Haifa.
Particulars: 17,951 gross tons; 622 × 76 × 28 feet.
Builders: Federal Shipbuilding & Dry Dock Co., Kearny, New Jersey, 1944.
Machinery: Steam turbines; twin screw; service speed 20 knots.
Capacity: 157 first class and 452 tourist class.
Notes: Former troopship rebuilt as a passenger ship; more money spent on this vessel in rebuilds and conversions than any other liner ever built.

August 6, 1944: Launched as *General W. P. Richardson*, U.S. Government troopship; (5,200 troops, 475 crew); cost $7 million. Original intention was to name her *General R. M. Blatchford.*
November 2, 1944: Commissioned for active duty.
February 1946: Transferred to U.S. Army for further trooping.
March 1948: Declared surplus and laid-up. Later chartered to American Export Lines, who offered to rebuild the ship for commercial service. Rebuilt at Ingalls Shipbuilding yard at Pascagoula, Mississippi; cost $5 million.
May 27, 1949: Left New York on first transatlantic crossing as *La Guardia.*
December 13, 1951: Returned to U.S. Maritime Commission as uneconomic.
1952: Made some transpacific trooping voyages for Korean War.
November 1952: Laid-up in James River, Virginia Reserve Fleet.
1956: Sold to Hawaiian Textron Lines, U.S. flag, for $3.5 million; then refitted for an additional $4 million; renamed *Leilani*. San Francisco–Honolulu cruise service; 650 one-class passengers.
January 1959: Laid-up; again uneconomic.

Renamed *Atlantis*, the former *President Roosevelt* awaits conversion and rebuilding in this 1970 photo. She had been American Export's *La Guardia*. (*Author's collection*)

The ex-*La Guardia* in her final days as the *Ocean Explorer 1*, laid-up in Greece. (*Author's collection*)

1960: Sold to American President Lines, U.S. flag; renamed *President Roosevelt*; rebuilt for $10 million by Puget Sound Bridge & Dry Dock Co., Seattle.
May 10, 1962: Maiden trans-Pacific cruise from San Francisco; tonnage relisted as 18,920; 456 all-first class passengers.
March 1970: Sold to Solon Navigation S/A (Chandris Group), Greek flag, for $1.8 million; renamed *Atlantis*. Rebuilt at Perama, Greece; tonnage increased to 24,458; capacity 1,092 one-class passengers.
June 1971: Maiden cruise for Chandris–America Lines: New York–Nassau–Freeport.
January 31, 1972: Sold to Eastern Steamship Lines with November delivery.
April 1972: Was to have been chartered to Cunard Line for New York–Bermuda cruise service; never materialized.
November 1972: Transferred to Eastern Steamship Lines, Panamanian flag (owned by Ares Shipping Corp and chartered to Eastern); renamed *Emerald Seas*. Miami–Nassau–Freeport service; 962 one-class passengers.
1984: Transferred to Easter Steamship Lines (Gotaas–Larsen Shipping Corp), Panamanian flag.
1987: Tonnage relisted as 18,927.
1990: Changed to Liberian flag.
1992: Sold to Seafest Cruises, Liberian flag; renamed *Funtastica* then *Fantastica*, *Terrifica*, and finally *Sapphire Seas*; charter cruises mostly.
1994–97: Laid-up at Piraeus.
1998: Used as hotel ship for Expo 98 at Lisbon; later sold to Excellence Holdings Ltd., Panamanian flag; renamed *Ocean Explorer I*; charter for world cruises; unsuccessful and with mechanical problems.
July 2001: Laid-up in Eleusis Bay.
2004: Sold to Indian scrappers; renamed *Explorer*.
December 1, 2004: Arrived at Alang under tow for demolition.

Excalibur

Service: New York to Barcelona, Marseilles, Naples, Alexandria, Beirut, Iskenderun (Turkey), Latakia (Syria), Beirut, Alexandria, Piraeus, Naples, Genoa, Marseilles, Barcelona and return to New York. Roundtrip forty-seven days. Itinerary later altered.
Particulars: 9,644 gross tons; 473 × 66 × 27 feet.
Builders: Bethlehem Steel Co., Sparrows Point, Maryland, 1944.
Machinery: Steam turbines; single screw; service speed 17 knots.
Capacity: 125 all-first class passengers.
Notes: These four sister ships were known as the "Four Aces" and were first fully air-conditioned passenger ships.

1944: Commissioned as transport *USS Duchess* for U.S. Navy; intended for sea invasion of Japan.
1944–47: Government service.
1947–48: Bought by American Export Lines, U.S. flag; renamed *Excalibur*; underwent conversion to passenger-cargo ship at New York.
September 24, 1948: Maiden voyage from New York to the Mediterranean.
June 27, 1950: Rammed Danish freighter *Colombia* in New York harbor; heavy damages; freighter caught fire and *Excalibur* grounded on Gowanus Flats, Brooklyn; later refloated and repaired.
June 1963: Fire at sea and returned to New York for repairs.
1965: Laid-up at Todd Shipyard, Hoboken; later sold to Atlantic Far East Lines (C. Y. Tung Group), Liberian flag; renamed *Oriental Jade*. San Francisco–Far East service.
January 22, 1974: Arrived at Kaohsiung, Taiwan for scrapping.

Excambion

Service: New York–Mediterranean (same ports as *Excalibur*).
Particulars: 9,644 gross tons; 473 × 66 × 27 feet.
Builders: Bethlehem Steel Co., Sparrows Point, Maryland, 1944.
Machinery: Steam turbines; single screw; service speed 17 knots.
Capacity: 125 all-first class passengers.

December 16, 1944: Commissioned as *USS Queens*, U.S. Navy transport.
1944–47: Government service.
1947: Sold to American Export Lines; renamed *Excambion*; began major rebuilding.
December 3, 1948: Departed from New York on maiden voyage to the Mediterranean.
1958: Made charter voyage to East Coast of South of America for Moore–McCormack Lines, U.S. flag.
1959: Laid-up in U.S. Federal Reserve Fleet in upper Hudson River.
1965: Transferred to Texas Aviation & Maritime University at Galveston, Texas; renamed *Texas Clipper*; refitted as cadet training ship.
1996–2006: Laid-up in Federal Reserve Fleet, Beaumont, Texas.
2006: Transferred to Texas Parks & Wildlife Department.
November 2007: Deliberately sunk as an artificial reef off Texas coast.

Bon Voyage: The *Excambion* makes a 4 p.m. departure from Jersey City. (*Author's collection*)

The 473-foot-long *Exeter* makes a visit to Baltimore. (*James McNamara collection*)

Exeter

Service: New York–Mediterranean (same ports as *Excalibur*).
Particulars: 9,644 gross tons; 473 × 66 × 27 feet.
Builders: Bethlehem Steel Co., Sparrows Point, Maryland, 1944.
Machinery: Steam turbines; single screw; service speed 17 knots.
Capacity: 125 all-first class passengers.
January 20, 1945: Commissioned as *USS Shelby*; attack transport for U.S. Navy.
1945–47: Military duties.
1947: Purchased by American Export Lines; renamed *Exeter;* rebuilt at New York.
December 1, 1948: Maiden sailing from New York to the Mediterranean.
1964: Laid-up at Todd Shipyard, Hoboken, New Jersey.
1965: Sold to Atlantic Far East Lines (C. Y. Tung Group), Liberian flag; renamed *Oriental Pearl*; San Francisco–Far East service.
1974: Scrapped at Kaohsiung, Taiwan.

Exochorda

Service: New York–Mediterranean (same ports as *Excalibur*).
Particulars: 9,644 gross tons; 473 × 66 × 27 feet.
Builders: Bethlehem Steel Co., Sparrows Point, Maryland, 1944.
Machinery: Steam turbines; single screw; service speed 17 knots.
Capacity: 125 all-first class passengers.
1944: Commissioned as *USS Dauphin*; U.S. Navy attack transport.

1944–47: Military work.
1947: Sold to American Export Lines; renamed *Exochorda;* rebuilt at New York.
November 2, 1948: Left New York on first voyage to the Mediterranean.
1959: Laid-up in U.S. Federal Reserve Fleet in upper Hudson River.
1967: Removed from Reserve Fleet; sold to Stevens Institute of Technology, Hoboken, New Jersey; converted to floating student dormitory by Bethlehem Steel Co., Hoboken; renamed *Stevens*; later moved to permanent berth in Hoboken.
August 1975: Towed to Chester, Pennsylvania for scrapping.
March 1979: Half-scrapped ship towed back to New York; partially scrapped at Jersey City and then Kearny, New Jersey.

Independence

Service: New York to Algeciras, Cannes, Genoa, and Naples; also cruising to the Caribbean and Mediterranean.
Particulars: 29,500 tons; after 1959, 30,293 gross tons; 683 × 89 × 30 feet.
Builders: Bethlehem Steel Co., Quincy, Massachusetts, 1951.
Machinery: Steam turbines; twin screw; service speed 23 knots.
Capacity: 295 first class, 375 cabin class, and 330 tourist class.
Notes: When completed, *Independence* was the fastest American liner.

March 19, 1949: Keel laid.
June 3, 1950: Launched.
January 1951: Speed trials 26½ knots.
February 11, 1951: Maiden sailing from New York: fifty-three-day Mediterranean cruise.
February–March 1959: Extensive refit at Newport News Shipyard in Virginia; 110 first class berths added.
1960: Repainted with white hull.
1968: Briefly operated by Fugazy Travel Service and repainted in bright, psychedelic colors for cruising: New York to the Caribbean and Mediterranean; uneconomical.

High 'n' Dry: The *Independence* takes a turn in dry dock at 56th Street, Brooklyn yard of Bethlehem Steel. (*Cronican-Arroyo collection*)

March 1969: Laid-up at Baltimore.
March 1974: Sold to Atlantic Far East Lines (C. Y. Tung Group), Liberian flag; renamed *Oceanic Independence*; sailed to Hong Kong and refitted.
1975: Cruising from Cape Town on charter; 950 one-class passengers.
January 19, 1976: Laid-up at Hong Kong.
March 1977: Renamed *Sea Luck I*; plan to become a floating hotel in the Middle East never materialized.
August 1979: Rumored to return to U.S. flag for California–Hawaii cruising.
December 1979: Renamed *Oceanic Independence*; began refit at Kobe, Japan, in preparation for Hawaiian cruise service.
June 1980: Placed under U.S. flag for American Hawaii Cruises.
June 21, 1980: First weekly cruise from Honolulu; 750 one-class passengers.
September 24, 1981: Aground off Nawiliwili, Kauai; ship damaged.
October 7, 1981: Sailed to San Francisco for full repairs.
1982: Transferred to American Global Line, U.S. flag; renamed *Independence*; continued in American Hawaii Cruises service.
1984: Registered at Honolulu.
May 1996: Extensive refit at Newport News Shipyard in Virginia.
October 2001: Collapse of American Hawaii Cruises.
November 2001: Ship moved to San Francisco and later placed in nearby Suisun Bay Federal Reserve Fleet.
February 2003: Rumored sale to Norwegian Cruise Lines, to be restored and reactivated along with United States for U.S.-flag cruising.
July 2004: Moved to San Francisco shipyard.
September 2005: Rumored to be used for housing at New Orleans following Hurricane Katrina.
2006: Renamed *Oceanic.*
August 2, 2008: Departed San Francisco under tow bound for Singapore and then Alang in India.
October 7, 2008: Reached Alang as *Platinum II*, but went aground and broke in two prior to being beached for scrapping; demolished where it laid.

Constitution

Service: New York–Mediterranean (ports same as *Independence*).
Particulars: 29,500 (later 30,293) gross tons; 683 × 89 × 30 feet.
Builders: Bethlehem Steel Co., Quincy, Massachusetts, 1951.
Machinery: Steam turbines; twin screw; service speed 23 knots.
Capacity: 295 first class, 375 cabin class, and 330 tourist class.
July 12, 1949: Keel laid.
September 16, 1950: Launched.
June 21, 1951: Left New York on maiden voyage to the Mediterranean.
January–February 1959 Feb: Extensive refit at Newport News Shipyard in Virginia; 110 first class berths added.
March 1, 1959: Collided outside New York harbor with Norwegian tanker *Jalanta;* tanker cut in two; *Constitution* damaged and repaired at Brooklyn.
1960: Repainted with a white hull.
1968: Cruising only.
September 1968: Laid-up at Jacksonville, Florida.
March 1974: Sold to Atlantic Far East Lines (C. Y. Tung Group), Liberian flag; renamed *Oceanic Constitution.*
April 26, 1974: Left Jacksonville under tow.
August 4, 1974: Arrived Hong Kong; laid-up.
August 1980: Rumored to be under consideration for California–Hawaii cruise service for American Hawaii Cruises, U.S. flag; intention would be for thorough refit and possible conversion to diesel propulsion; reintroduction would be in 1982.
1981: Transferred to American Hawaii Cruises; extensive refit at Kaohsiung.
June 1982: Transferred to American Global Line (C. Y. Tung Group); renamed *Constitution*; began cruising from Honolulu.

The *Constitution* docking at New York's Pier 84 in 1960. (*Anton Logvinenko*)

Between Piers: The *Atlantic* being shifted between Piers 84 and 86 at New York. (*Author's collection*)

1984: Registered in Honolulu.
1996: Laid-up at Portland, Oregon; proposed major refit never materialized.
November 17, 1997: Sank off Hawaiian Islands while empty and under tow; bound for Chinese scrappers.

Atlantic (1953)

Service: New York to Algeciras, Naples, Messina, Piraeus, and Haifa; periodic changes in itinerary; off-season cruising.
Particulars: 14,138 gross tons; 564 × 76 × 28 feet.
Builders: Sun Shipbuilding & Dry Dock Co., Chester, Pennsylvania, 1953.
Machinery: Steam turbines; single screw; service speed 20 knots.
Capacity: Forty first class and 840 tourist class.
Notes: Former freighter rebuilt as a passenger ship. After refit in 1960, this ship had the largest outdoor swimming pool afloat.

1953–57: Built as freighter *Badger Mariner*; then rebuilt as *Atlantic* for American Banner Lines (qv).
October 1959: Purchased by American Export Lines; refitted at Sun Shipbuilding & Dry Dock Co., Chester, Pennsylvania.
May 16, 1960: Maiden sailing for American Export Lines from New York to the Mediterranean.
April 1965: Restyled as an all-tourist class: 840 tourist class passengers.
October 1967: Withdrawn and laid-up at Brooklyn.
May 1968: Planned to become trade ship displaying American goods; to be renamed *Atlantic World Trade Ship*; never materialized.
March 1969: Moved to Baltimore; still laid-up.
1971: Sold to Seawise Foundations Inc. (C. Y. Tung Group), Liberian flag; sale price $2.4 million; renamed *Universe Campus*; refitted as educational cruise ship.
September 1971: Commenced first educational cruise with teachers and students.
1976: Renamed *Universe*; laid-up at San Francisco.
1977: Began regular cruising from North American ports.
1984: Transferred to Island Navigation Corp. (C. Y. Tung Group); capacity reduced to 554.
1992–95: Plagued with mechanical problems.
1995: Laid-up.
1996: Towed to Alang, India, and scrapped.

Nuclear Power: Maiden arrival of the innovative *Savannah* at New York. (*ALF collection*)

Savannah

Service: Goodwill demonstration voyages from New York to ports around the world; later from New York to Mediterranean and North European ports.
Particulars: 13,599 gross tons; 595 × 78 × 29 feet.
Builders: New York Shipbuilding Co., Camden, New Jersey, 1958–62.
Machinery: Nuclear reactor plus turbines; single screw; service speed 20 knots.
Capacity: Sixty first-class passengers.
Notes: World's first nuclear-powered merchant ship.

May 22, 1958: Keel laid; sponsored by Mrs. Richard Nixon.
July 21, 1959: Launched by Mrs. Dwight Eisenhower.
December 1961–April 1962: Special extended sea trials; total cost $53 million.
May 1962: Assigned to States Marine Lines, U.S. flag, for operational management; owned by U.S. Government; sailed in worldwide goodwill voyages.
1964: Assigned to New York–Mediterranean service.
August 1965: Management transferred to American Export Lines (FAST—First Atomic Ship Transport); commercially unsuccessful.
1966: Ceased carrying passengers.
February 1969: Offered for charter.
1970: Laid-up at Galveston, Texas.
January 10, 1972: Laid-up at Savannah, Georgia.
1981: Moved to Charleston, South Carolina.
1994–2004: Laid-up in Federal Reserve Fleet, James River, Virginia.
May 2008: Arrived under tow at Baltimore with intention of using ship as museum.

3

American President Lines

President Monroe

Service: Continuous around-the-world sailings: New York to Cristobal, Balboa, Acapulco, San Francisco, Honolulu, Yokohama, Kobe, Hong Kong, Singapore, Singapore, Penang, Colombo, Cochin, Bombay, Karachi, Suez, Port Said, Alexandria, Naples, Marseilles, Genoa, Leghorn, and New York. Transatlantic passengers carried on westbound Mediterranean–New York portion.
Particulars: 9,235 gross tons; 492 × 70 × 27 feet.
Builders: Newport News Shipbuilding & Dry Dock Co., Newport News, Virginia, 1940.
Machinery: Steam turbines; single screw; service speed 16½ knots.
Capacity: Ninety-six first-class passengers.

December 28, 1940: Maiden voyage: New York–Panama–California–Bombay–Cape Town–New York (ninety-five days).
December 1941: Chartered to War Shipping Administration; military service.
July 1943–November 1946: Chartered to U.S. Army.
November 25, 1946: Left New York on first post-war world voyage.
December 1965: Withdrawn from American President service; laid-up.
1966: Sold to White Star Shipping & Trading Co. (John S. Latsis Line), Greek flag; sale price $650,000; renamed *Marianna V*. General Mediterranean and tramping services without passengers.
June 26, 1969: Arrived at Hong Kong for scrapping.

President Polk

Service: Continuous around-the-world voyages (ports same as *President Monroe*).
Particulars: 9,260 gross tons; 492 × 70 × 27 feet.
Builders: Newport News Shipbuilding & Dry Dock Co., Newport News, Virginia, 1940.

The *President Polk* berthed at Boston. (*Alex Duncan*)

Machinery: Steam turbines; single screw; service speed 16½ knots.
Capacity: Ninety-six first-class passengers.

November 6, 1940: Departed New York on maiden voyage to Panama and California.
December 1941–September 1943: Chartered to U.S. War Shipping Administration; military service.
September 1943–August 1946: Chartered to U.S. Navy.
August 13, 1946: Departed New York on first post-war world voyage.
December 1965: Withdrawn from service and briefly laid-up. Sold to Ganaderos del Mar S/A, Liberian flag; sale price $650,000; renamed *Gaucho Martin Fierro*; refitted as cattle carrier.
1966: Renamed *Minotaurus*.
1970: Scrapped at Kaohsiung, Taiwan.

4

Arosa Line

Arosa Kulm

Service: Montreal (from Halifax in winter) to Southampton, Zeebrugge, and Bremerhaven; numerous alterations in scheduling including occasional voyages from New York.
Particulars: 8,929 gross tons; 448 × 58 × 26 feet.
Builders: American International Shipbuilding Corp, Hog Island, Pennsylvania, 1920.
Machinery: Steam turbines; single screw; service speed 14½ knots.
Capacity: Forty-six first-class and 919 tourist class; later changed to twenty first and 945 tourist; and finally to thirty first and 802 tourist.
Notes: Former freighter rebuilt as a passenger ship.

1920: Launched by visiting King Albert of Belgium as Hog Island-type transport *Cantigny.*
1924: Sold to United States Lines; rebuilt as combination passenger-cargo ship *American Banker*; sixty-five one-class passengers (later increased to eighty-five). New York–London service.
1940: Owing to American neutrality and eruption of war in Europe, ship transferred to Antwerp Navigation Co; renamed *Ville d'Anvers.*
1940–46: Wartime service as a freighter.
1946: Returned to United States Lines and then transferred to Luckenbach Line, Honduran flag; later transferred to Sociedad Naviera Transatlantic, Panamanian flag; rebuilt as migrant ship *City of Athens.*
1947: Seized for debt and auctioned-off to Panamanian Lines, Panamanian flag; renamed *Protea*; migrant sailings.
1949: Ownership changed to Compañía de Operaciones Maritima, Panamanian flag; migrant sailings from Mediterranean ports.
1951: Chartered to Incres Line for three transatlantic sailings: Antwerp–Plymouth–Montreal. Then sold to Arosa Line, Panamanian flag; renamed *Arosa Kulm*; rebuilt at Bremerhaven for low-fare tourist service.
March 1952: Inaugurated Arosa Line service to Montreal.
November 1958: Charter voyage West Indies–U.K.
December 1958: Following collapse of Arosa Line seized for debt at Plymouth.
May 7, 1959: Arrived at Bruges for scrapping.

Arosa Star

Service: Bremerhaven–Le Havre–Southampton–Quebec City and/or Montreal; periodic changes in scheduling including voyages to Halifax and/or New York; off-season cruises.
Particulars: 9,070 gross tons; 466 × 60 × 23 feet.
Builders: Bethlehem Steel Co., Quincy, Massachusetts, 1931.
Machinery: Steam turbines; single screw; service speed 15 knots.
Capacity: Thirty-eight first class and 768 tourist class.

1931–41: Sailed as *Borinquen,* New York & Porto Rico Steamship Co., U.S. flag; New York–San Juan–Ciudad Trujillo service; 261 first class and ninety-six second-class passengers.
1942–46: U.S. Government trooping.
1946–49: Refitted and resumed New York–Caribbean service, but for Agwilines, U.S. flag.
1949: Sold to Bull Line, U.S. flag; renamed *Puerto Rico*; New York–Caribbean service.
March 1953: Laid-up in Brooklyn; offered for sale.
January 1954: Sold to Arosa Line, Panamanian flag; renamed *Arosa Star*; refitted at Bremerhaven for $1 million; capacity increased to 806.
May 18, 1954: Maiden voyage for Arosa Line: Bremerhaven–Quebec City.
December 7, 1958: Following collapse of Arosa Line, ship seized at Bermuda for debt.

The *Arosa Kulm* berthed at the 9th Street pier in Hoboken. (*Gillespie-Faber collection*)

The *Arosa Star* stops at Tilbury-London. (*Author's collection*)

1959: Sold to McCormick Shipping Corp, Panamanian flag, for $510,000; renamed *Bahama Star*; refitted at Jacksonville. Operated by Eastern Steamship Lines; Miami–Nassau cruise service.
November 1965: Rescued survivors from burning cruise ship *Yarmouth Castle* in passage between Florida and the Bahamas.
November 1968: Withdrawn; laid-up.
1969: Rumored to be sold to Central American buyers to become a floating hotel; instead sold to Western Steamship Co., Panamanian flag; renamed *La Janelle*; to become a floating hotel along California coast.
April 13, 1970: Became a total loss during hurricane; beached at Port Hueneme, California; capsized and later scrapped on the spot.

Arosa Sun

Service: Bremerhaven–Le Havre–Southampton–Quebec City and/or Montreal. Periodic other voyages to New York. Winter cruising.
Particulars: 20,126 gross tons; 598 × 68 × 33 feet.
Builders: Ateliers et Chantiers de la Loire, Saint-Nazaire, France, 1931.
Machinery: Sulzer diesels; twin screw; service speed 16½ knots.
Capacity: 100 first class and 949 tourist class.
December 17, 1929: Launched as *Félix Roussel* for Messageries Maritimes, French flag.
February 26, 1931: Left Marseilles on maiden voyage to the Far East via Suez.
1936: Lengthened from 568 to 598 feet; re-engined.
1940–46: Allied trooping; managed by the Bibby Line, British flag.
April 15, 1946: Decommissioned at Durban; returned to Messageries Maritimes.
June 1948–September 1950: Major refit at Dunkirk; single stack replaced former twin stacks; afterward returned to Marseilles–Far East service.
April 1955: Sold to Arosa Line, Panamanian flag, for $3.5 million; refitted at Trieste; renamed *Arosa Sun*.
July 1955: Maiden voyage for Arosa Line: Trieste–Palermo–Naples–Lisbon–New York–Quebec City–Le Havre–Southampton–Bremerhaven.
August 1955: Hereafter sailings Bremerhaven to Canada mostly.
March 15, 1958: Engine room explosion off Colombia during Caribbean cruise.
December 1958: Following collapse of Arosa Line arrested for debt at Bremerhaven; laid-up.
1959: Reportedly sold to Grimaldi-Siosa Lines; never materialized.
September 1960: Sold to Koninklijke Nederlandsche Hoogovens en Staalfabrieken, Holland.

In her final years, the *Arosa Sun* was a moored accommodation ship for workers in a Dutch steel mill. (*ALF collection*)

Maiden Arrival: The *Arosa Sky* arrives at New York for the first time in May 1957. (*ALF collection*)

February 1961: Began use as permanently moored accommodation at steel works at IJmuiden, Holland.
April 9, 1963: Damaged by fire.
March 28, 1974: Arrived at Bilbao under tow from IJmuiden for scrapping.

Arosa Sky

Service: Bremerhaven–Le Havre–Southampton–Halifax (westbound only)–New York. Winter cruising and charter voyages as well.
Particulars: 17,408 gross tons; 594 × 75 × 26 feet.
Builders: Société Provençale de Constructions Navales, La Ciotat, France, 1948–49.
Machinery: Sulzer diesels; twin screw; service speed 21 knots.
Capacity: Sixty-four first class and 834 tourist class.

1939: Keel laid; then construction interrupted by war.
June 16, 1944: Launched as *Marechal Petain*.
August 1944: Sunk by Nazi occupation forces.
1946: Raised and towed to Toulon for completion; renamed *La Marseillaise*.
August 18, 1949: Maiden voyage for Messageries Maritimes, French flag; Marseilles–Far East service.
February 1957: Sold to Arosa Line, Panamanian flag, for $6½ million; renamed *Arosa Sky*; refitted.
May 10, 1957: Maiden voyage: Bremerhaven–Le Havre–Southampton–Halifax–New York.
January 8, 1958: Fire in passenger cabins off Wilmington, North Carolina, during Caribbean cruise.
October 1958: Sold to Costa Line, Italian flag, for $8 million; renamed *Bianca C.*
1958–59: Major refit; modernized; tonnage relisted as 18,427.
1959: Genoa-West Indies service; also cruising from New York to the Caribbean.
October 22, 1961: Gutted by fire off Grenada, British West Indies; sank in deep water on October 24.

5

Baltic Steamship Co.

Alexandr Pushkin

Service: Seasonal April–October: Leningrad, Bremerhaven, London, Le Havre, to Montreal. Occasional cruising.
Particulars: 19,860 gross tons; 577 × 77 × 27 feet.
Builders: Mathias-Thesen-Werft, Wismar, East Germany, 1965.
Machinery: Sulzer diesels; twin screw; service speed 20 knots.
Capacity: Eighty-six first class and 580 tourist class; later changed to 680 one-class.
Notes: First Soviet passenger liner to operate a regular Atlantic service since the late 1940s and the first regular Soviet passenger service to Canada.

May 26, 1964: Launched.
June 1965: Maiden cruise.
April 18, 1966: Maiden transatlantic crossing to Montreal.
1974–75: Refitted for further cruising. Tonnage relisted as 20,502.
1981: Transatlantic service discontinued; cruising only hereafter.
1985: Transferred to Far East Shipping Co., Vladivostok.
1990: To be refitted at Singapore for further cruising; never materialized.
1991: Sold to Orient Line, Bahamian flag; renamed *Marco Polo.*
1991–93: Major refit at Syros, Greece.
1993: Began cruising; 850 one-class passengers; worldwide cruising.
January 2010: Began cruising for Cruise & Maritime Voyages.
2015: Reached fiftieth year.
2017: Operation extended to 2019.

Mikhail Lermontov

Service: May–October: Leningrad, Bremerhaven, London, and Le Havre to New York. Otherwise cruising.
Particulars: 19,872 gross tons; 578 × 77 × 27 feet.
Builders: Mathias-Thesen-Werft Shipyard, Wismar, East Germany, 1971.
Machinery: Sulzer diesels; twin screw; service speed 20 knots.
Capacity: 700 one-class passengers.
Notes: The first Soviet liner to offer regular service to New York since the late 1940s.

December 31, 1970: Launched.
April 1972: Maiden voyage: Cruise from Bremerhaven to Canary Islands.
June 19, 1972: Arrived at Montreal on first Atlantic crossing.
May 1973: Began sailings to New York.
September–October 1980: Refitted and upgraded for further cruising.
1980: Cruising only hereafter.
1981: Transatlantic service discontinued.
January–May 1982: Major refit at Bremerhaven; accommodation improved and modernized; hull repainted all-white.
February 16, 1986: Sank after striking rocks off South Island, New Zealand.

The *Alexandr Pushkin* later became the popular cruise ship *Marco Polo*. (*Tim Noble collection*)

In later years, the *Mikhail Lermontov* was repainted in white and mostly used for cruising. (*Mick Lindsay collection*)

6

Canadian Pacific Steamships

Empress of France

Service: April–December: Liverpool and Greenock to Quebec City and Montreal (to Saint John, NB in winter).
Particulars: 20,448 gross tons; 601 × 75 × 27 feet.
Builders: John Brown & Co. Ltd., Clydebank, Scotland, 1928.
Machinery: Steam turbines; twin screw; service speed 18 knots.
Capacity: 400 first class and 300 tourist class. After 1958–59 refit: 218 first class and 482 tourist class.

January 24, 1928: Launched.
June 1, 1928: Maiden voyage Liverpool–Montreal as *Duchess of Bedford*.
1928–39: Summer service: Liverpool–Belfast–Greenock–Quebec City–Montreal; winter cruises from Liverpool and New York to the Caribbean and Mediterranean.
January 1933: Began four months charter to Furness–Bermuda Line for New York–Bermuda sailings.
August 1939: Requisitioned for trooping; first voyage Liverpool–Bombay.
1939–47: War service; afterward refitted.
September 1, 1948: Returned to Liverpool–Montreal service as *Empress of France* (original intention was *Empress of India*).
January 1959: Given new, more modern funnels; accommodation changes.
December 7, 1960: Completed 338th and final Canadian Pacific voyage at Liverpool; sold to be scrapped at Newport, Monmouthshire.

Empress of Canada (1928)

Service: Liverpool–Montreal (same ports as *Empress of Canada*).
Particulars: 20,235 gross tons; 600 × 75 × 27 feet.
Builders: John Brown & Co. Ltd. Clydebank, Scotland, 1928.
Machinery: Steam turbines; twin screw; service speed 18 knots.
Capacity: 400 first class and 300 tourist class.

June 1928: Launched as *Duchess of Richmond*.
March 15, 1929: Departed Liverpool to maiden voyage to Saint John NB; later sailings to Quebec City and Montreal with winter cruising from New York and Liverpool.
1939–46: Trooping.
May 1946: Commenced major refit; renamed *Empress of Canada*.
July 16, 1947: Left Liverpool on post-war maiden voyage to Quebec City and Montreal.
January 25, 1953: Gutted by fire and then capsized at Liverpool berth.
March 6, 1954: Refloated.
September 1, 1954: Left Liverpool under tow for scrapping at La Spezia.

Burned out and capsized, the *Empress of Canada* at her Liverpool berth in January 1953. (*Author's collection*)

Empress of Scotland

Service: Liverpool and Greenock to Quebec City (later extended to Montreal). Winter cruising from New York to the Caribbean.
Particulars: 26,313 gross tons; 666 × 83 × 31 feet.
Builders: Fairfield Shipbuilding & Engineering Co., Glasgow, Scotland, 1930.
Machinery: Steam turbines; twin screw; service speed 21 knots.
Capacity: 458 first class and 250 tourist class.
Notes: Fastest trans-Pacific liner 1930–39.

December 17, 1929: Launched as *Empress of Japan.*
June 1930: Special maiden voyage: Liverpool–Quebec City.
August 1930: Southampton to Vancouver via Suez and Hong Kong; thence regular trans-Pacific service between Vancouver, Victoria, and the Far East.
April 1931: Record run from Yokohama to Victoria of seven days, twenty hours, and sixteen minutes.
August 1939: Requisitioned for war duties as a troopship.
October 1942: Renamed *Empress of Scotland* prompted by Japan's entry into the war.
1948: Released from war service; commenced reconditioning.
May 9, 1950: Maiden post-war sailing from Liverpool to Quebec City.
November 1951: Carried Princess Elizabeth (later HM the Queen) and the Duke of Edinburgh from Portugal Cove NF to Liverpool.
May 1952: Masts shortened by 40 feet so as to proceed to Montreal.
November 8, 1957: Began final Canadian Pacific round voyage.
December 1957: Laid-up at Liverpool; then at Belfast.
January 1958: Sold to Hamburg–Atlantic Line, West German flag, for $2.8 million; provisionally renamed *Scotland* then changed to *Hanseatic* (qv).

Above: Regal Stance: The splendid *Empress of Scotland* at Liverpool. (*Mick Lindsay collection*)

Below: The splendid looking *Empress of Scotland* on post-war trials. (*Author's collection*)

The migrant ship *Beaverbrae*. (*Author's collection*)

Beaverbrae

Service: Westbound migrant service: Bremen-Saint John NB; eastbound operations mostly as a freighter.
Particulars: 9,034 gross tons; 469 × 60 × 21 feet.
Builders: Blohm & Voss A/G, Hamburg, Germany, 1939.
Machinery: Diesel-electric engines; single screw; service speed 16 knots.
Capacity: 775 one-class passengers.

December 15, 1938: Launched as *Huascaran* for Hamburg–America Line, German flag; thirty-two first-class passengers.
1939: Hamburg–West Coast of South America service.
1939–45: Used as a Nazi submarine depot ship.
May 1945: Seized by Allied invasion forces; later allocated to Canada.
September 2, 1947: Bought by Canadian Pacific Steamships Ltd., British flag from Canadian War Reparations Commission; rebuilt as migrant ship at Sorel, Quebec.
February 1948: Renamed *Beaverbrae.*
February 25, 1948: Commenced Bremen–Saint John service.
1948–54: Low-fare migrant service.
November 1, 1954: Sold to Cogedar Line, Italian flag; renamed *Aurelia* (qv).

Empress of Australia

Service: Liverpool–Montreal (same as *Empress of Canada).*
Particulars: 19,370 gross tons; 574 × 71 × 29 feet.
Builders: Cammell Laird & Co., Birkenhead, England, 1924.
Machinery: Steam turbines; twin screw; service speed 16 knots.
Capacity: 220 first class and 444 tourist class.

1924–53: Sailed as *De Grasse*, French Line (qv).
March 1953: Sold to Canadian Pacific Steamships Ltd., British flag; emergency replacement for fire-gutted *Empress of Canada.*
April 27, 1953: Renamed *Empress of Australia.*
April 28, 1953: Maiden sailing from Liverpool.
December 5, 1955: Sailed from Quebec City on final Canadian Pacific voyage.
January 9, 1956: Departed from Liverpool for Gareloch; laid-up.
February 15, 1956: Sold to Grimaldi-Siosa Lines, Italian flag; renamed *Venezuela* for Genoa–West Indies–Venezuela migrant service. Reconditioned and tonnage relisted as 18,567.
1960: Major refit: New bow added, increasing length to 614 feet; tonnage revised to 18,769; passenger accommodation restyled as 180 first class, 500 tourist class and 800 third class.
March 17, 1962: Grounded at Cannes.
April 16, 1962: Refloated; beyond economic repair.
August 26, 1962: Sold to be scrapped at La Spezia, Italy.

Empress of Britain

Service: Liverpool–Montreal (ports as for *Empress of Canada);* winter cruising—New York to the Caribbean and later from Liverpool and Southampton.
Particulars: 25,516 grt; 640 × 85 × 29 feet.
Builders: Fairfield Shipbuilding & Engineering Co., Glasgow, Scotland, 1956.
Machinery: Steam turbines; twin screw; service speed 20 knots.

Capacity: 160 first class and 894 tourist class.
Notes: First British liner to be completely air-conditioned.

September 30, 1953: Laid down.
June 22, 1955: Launched by Her Majesty Queen Elizabeth II.
April 20, 1956: Left Liverpool on maiden voyage to Montreal.
1963–64: Considerable off-season cruising from Liverpool, Southampton, Cape Town, etc.
February 18, 1964: Offered for sale; later same month sold to Greek Line; renamed *Queen Anna Maria* (qv).

Empress of England

Service: Liverpool–Montreal (same as for *Empress of Canada*). Winter cruising from New York and later from Liverpool and Southampton.
Particulars: 25,585 gross tons; 640 × 85 × 29 feet.
Builders: Vickers-Armstrong Shipbuilders Ltd., Newcastle-upon-Tyne, England, 1957.
Machinery: Steam turbines; twin screw; service speed 20 knots.
Capacity: 160 first class and 898 tourist class.

December 22, 1954: Keel laid; rumor that this ship would be named *Empress of Wales*.
May 9, 1955: Launched by Lady Eden as *Empress of England*.
April 18, 1957: Departed Liverpool on maiden crossing to Montreal.
November 8, 1965: Collided with tanker *Lifjord* off Quebec City.
December 1968: Repainted in new Canadian Pacific colors.
April 1970: Sold to Shaw Savill Line, British flag; intended name *Pacific Empress*, but changed to *Ocean Monarch*; made one round voyage to Australia.
October 1970: Given $12 million refit for cruising; made one-class; refit long delayed and troubled.
October 16, 1971: Maiden cruise; 1,372 one-class passengers; tonnage relisted as 25,971.
1973: Full year of Pacific cruising from Australian ports.
June 1975: Withdrawn from service.
June 13, 1975: Left Southampton to be scrapped at Kaohsiung.
July 17, 1975: Arrived Kaohsiung.
December 10, 1975: Demolition began.

Empress of Canada (1961)

Service: Liverpool and Greenock to Quebec City and Montreal; winter cruising from New York to the Caribbean and Mediterranean.

Second Careers: The *Mardi Gras* (ex-*Empress of Canada*) passes the *Carnivale* (ex-*Empress of Britain*) at Miami. (*Rich Turnwald collection*

Shaw Savill's *Ocean Monarch*, the former *Empress of England*, seen at Melbourne. (*Tim Noble collection*)

Particulars: 27,284 gross tons; 650 × 87 × 29 feet.
Builders: Vickers-Armstrong Shipbuilders Ltd., Newcastle-upon-Tyne, England, 1961.
Machinery: Steam turbines; twin screw; service speed 20 knots.
Capacity: 200 first class and 856 tourist class; 650 one-class for cruising.
Notes: The final Canadian Pacific liner.

January 27, 1959: Keel laid.
May 10, 1960: Launched by Mrs. John Diefenbaker.
April 24, 1961: Departed Liverpool on maiden voyage to Montreal.
November 1968: End of Canadian Pacific service to Greenock; thereafter sailings direct from Liverpool.
December 1968: Repainted in new Canadian Pacific colors.
November 27, 1969: First sailing from Southampton.
September 3, 1970: First cruise from Montreal: to Saguenay, Boston and Bermuda (fourteen days)
November 23, 1971: Withdrawn from service; termination of Canadian Pacific's liner operations.

Alongside at Liverpool: The *Empress of Canada* with the Swedish *Kungsholm* just behind. (*ALF collection*)

After 1968, the *Empress of Canada* had a new paint scheme. (*Rich Turnwald collection*)

December 17, 1971: Laid-up at Tilbury.
January 1972: Sold to Carnival Cruise Lines, Panamanian flag, for $6 million; renamed *Mardi Gras*.
February 26, 1972: Sailed from Tilbury to Miami to begin seven-day Caribbean cruise service. Carnival's first ship.
1990: Registered in the Bahamas.
1991: Capacity relisted as 1,106.
September 1993 Sep: Sold to Royal Olympic Cruises, Greek flag; renamed *Olympic*.
1994: Used for gambling cruises from Galveston as *Star of Texas*; later gambling cruises from Miami as *Lucky Star*.
1995: Returned to Royal Olympic Cruises; renamed *Olympic*.
1997: Used for Direct Holidays charter; major refit.
1998: Renamed *Apollon*.
1999–2000: Chartered to First Choice Cruises.
2000: Returned to Royal Olympic Cruises; laid-up at Piraeus.
2001: Reactivated for seasonal three- to four-day cruises from Piraeus.
2003: Laid-up.
December 4, 2003: Arrived at Alang to be scrapped.

7

Chandris Lines

Queen Frederica

Service: Summer season sailings between Piraeus, Messina, Naples, and New York; also cruising. Periodic sailings from Southampton to Australia via Suez and also full around-the-world voyages returning to Southampton via Panama.
Particulars: 16,435 gross tons; 582 × 83 × 29 feet.
Builders: William Cramp & Sons Ship & Engine Building Co., Camden, New Jersey, 1927.
Machinery: Steam turbines; twin screw; service speed 21 knots.
Capacity: 174 first class and 1,005 tourist class; often merged into one-class. 650 one-class for cruising from New York.

1927–37: Sailed as *Malolo,* Matson Navigation Co., U.S. flag.
1937–48: Renamed *Matsonia,* Matson Navigation Co., U.S. flag.
1948: Sold to Home Lines, Panamanian flag; renamed *Atlantic* (qv).
December 1954: Transferred to National Hellenic American Line, Greek flag; renamed *Queen Frederica* (qv).
November 1965: Sold to Chandris Group (Themistocles Navigation S/A), Greek flag. First Chandris sailing: Southampton–Australia.

The veteran *Queen Frederica* loads at Southampton. (*Mick Lindsay collection*)

March 21, 1966: Arrived in New York on first Chandris crossing.
September 1967: Final transatlantic crossing.
November 4, 1969: Damaged by fire while on a voyage Villefranche-sur-Mer–Piraeus.
1971: Laid-up in River Dart, England.
January 28, 1972: Aground in the River Dart; later refloated.
1973: Chartered to Sun Cruises for twenty-seven seven-day Mediterranean cruises from Cannes.
November 5, 1973: Laid-up at Perama, Greece.
May 1977: Sold to Greek shipbreakers.
February 1, 1978: Gutted by fire while being scrapped at Eleusis.

Ellinis

Service: Periodic eastbound crossings from New York to Southampton as part of full around-the-world voyages: Southampton, Piraeus, Port Said (or via Cape Town) Fremantle, Melbourne, Sydney, Auckland, Papeete, Panama, occasionally New York, and return to Southampton. Occasional cruising from New York, Southampton, and Sydney.
Particulars: 24,351 gross tons; 642 × 79 × 28 feet.
Builders: Bethlehem Steel Co., Quincy, Massachusetts, 1932.
Machinery: Steam turbines; twin screw; service speed 20 knots.
Capacity: 1,642 all-tourist class passengers.

July 18, 1932: Launched as *Lurline* for Matson Navigation Co., U.S. flag. Cost $8 million.
January 27, 1933: Maiden voyage.
1933–41: San Francisco–Honolulu service.
1942–46: Wartime troopship.
1947–48: Post-war refit and restoration; cost $21 million.

The *Ellinis* of Chandris Lines had been the *Lurline*, a longtime favorite on the Hawaiian run. (*Mick Lindsay collection*)

April 1948: Resumed San Francisco–Honolulu service.
September 1963: Sold Chandris Group (Marfuerza Cía Maritima S/A), Greek flag; renamed *Ellinis*. Major refit at Smith's Dock Co., North Shields; lengthened from 632 to 642 feet; passenger capacity increased from 761 to 1,642.
December 21, 1963: Left Tyneside for Australia on maiden voyage for Chandris.
October 21, 1968: First visit to New York for Chandris; then to Southampton.
March 1969: Struck by 40-foot wave in North Atlantic during New York–Southampton crossing.
October 1973: Final New York–Southampton crossing; thereafter, mostly cruising.
June 25, 1974: Arrived at Rotterdam and had a turbine replaced by one from her former sister *Homeric* (ex-*Mariposa*), which had been sold for scrap in late 1973.
December 1975: Based at Cape Town for cruising.
1977: Ownership changed to Australia Line S/A (Chandris Group), still Greek flag.
1981: Summer Mediterranean cruises from Genoa; laid-up in winter.
October 1981: Laid-up in Perama Bay.
1986: Sold for scrap; furnishings and engine parts removed and some used in original sister ship *Britanis* (ex-*Monterey*, ex-*Matsonia*, ex-*Lurline*).
1987: Scrapped at Kaohsiung, Taiwan.

Australis

Service: Eastbound sailings from Port Everglades to Southampton and occasionally to Rotterdam and Bremerhaven as part of continuous around-the-world service (Bremerhaven, Rotterdam, Southampton, Casablanca, Las Palmas, Cape Town (or through the Mediterranean via Gibraltar, Naples, Malta, Piraeus, Port Said and Aden) to Fremantle, Melbourne, Sydney, Auckland, Suva, Tahiti, Acapulco, Balboa, Cristobal, Port Everglades, and Southampton).
Particulars: 34,449 gross tons; 723 × 93 × 32 feet.
Builders: Newport News Shipbuilding & Dry Dock Co., Newport News, Virginia, 1940.
Machinery: Steam turbines; twin screw; service speed 22 knots.
Capacity: 2,258 one-class passengers.

1940–64: Service as *America*, United States Lines, U.S. flag (qv): and 1941–46 as *USS West Point*
November 1964: Sold to Okeania S/A (Chandris Group), Panamanian flag; renamed *Australis;* major refit at Piraeus and passenger capacity increased from 1,046 to 2,258.
August 20, 1965: Maiden voyage: Piraeus–Sydney.
October 1965: Commenced around-the-world service.
1968: Repainted with grey hull (it had been white); later transferred to Greek flag.
October 22, 1970: Damaged by galley fire while sailing between Auckland and Suva.

Flagship of Chandris Lines, the imposing *Australis* is between voyages at Southampton. (*Mick Lindsay collection*)

Broken in Half: The former *Australis* makes a very sad sight in this view from 2005. (*Stephen L. Tacey collection*)

November 18, 1977: Departed from Southampton on final voyage to Australia.
January 1978: Laid-up at Timaru, New Zealand; later sold for $5 million to America Cruise Lines (also called Venture Cruise Lines), remained under Greek flag; renamed *America.*
May 1978: Sailed to New York for new owners.
June 30, 1978: Sailed from New York on first short cruise; unsuccessful; arrested for debt on July 8.
July–August 1978: Laid-up at Pier 92, New York.
August 28, 1978: Auctioned-off by U.S. District Court; resold to Chandris for $1 million; sailed to Perama and laid-up.
March 1979: Renamed *Italis*; refit and forward funnel removed.
April 1979: Mediterranean cruising.
September 12, 1979: Laid-up in Perama Bay.
May 1980: Sold to Noga International Corp., Panamanian flag; renamed *Noga*; intended use as floating hotel never materialized.
1984: Sold to Silver Moon Ferries Ltd., Panamanian flag; renamed *Alferdoss*; further plans to use the ship never materialized.
September 1984: Flooding while laid-up; later beached and repaired; continued in lay-up.
1988: Variously rumored to become a floating hotel, yacht club, accommodation center and floating prison. Later sold for $2 million for scrap; some parts removed, but deal collapsed.
February 1993: Sold to Thai buyers to become a five-star hotel at Phuket.
August 1993: Renamed *American Star*.
December 31, 1993: Left Piraeus under tow for Phuket via South Africa.
January 1994: Caught in fierce eastern Atlantic storm.
January 17, 1994: Towlines snapped and ship adrift.
January 18, 1994: Ran aground on Fuerteventura, Canary Islands.
January 20, 1994: Broke in half.
1996: Stern section collapsed and fell into the sea.
April 2007: Forward section collapsed into the sea.

Caribbean Waters: The *Amerikanis* was a popular cruise ship. (*Author's collection*)

Amerikanis

Service: Occasional voyages: Piraeus, Messina, Naples, Gibraltar, New York. Mostly cruising from New York and other U.S. East Coast ports.
Particulars: 19,377 gross tons; 576 × 74 × 28 feet.
Builders: Harland & Wolff Ltd., Belfast, Northern Ireland, 1952.
Machinery: Steam turbines; twin screw; service speed 19 knots.
Capacity: 910 passengers in first and tourist class.

June 21, 1951: Launched as *Kenya Castle*, Union-Castle Line, British flag.
April 4, 1952: Departed from London on maiden voyage around Africa; 526 all cabin class passengers.
May–July 1961: Major refit; given dome on funnel; accommodation improved.
May 22, 1967: Laid-up in River Blackwater, England; later sold to National Hellenic American Line S/A (Chandris Group), Greek flag; renamed *Amerikanis.*
August 12, 1967: Arrived at Piraeus for extensive rebuilding.
August 8, 1968: Left Piraeus on maiden crossing to New York.
1970: Hereafter mostly cruising.
July 26, 1973: Struck submerged object off Bermuda; damaged but later repaired.
1975: Caribbean cruises from San Juan in winter; Mediterranean cruises from Genoa in summer.
1980: Began summer cruises from Amsterdam to North Cape and Northern cities.
1980: Transferred to Chandris-America Line, Liberian flag.
1981: Transferred to Costa Line management for Miami-Bahamas cruises; later returned to Chandris operation.
1984: Transferred to Fifth Transoceanic Shipping Co. Ltd. (Chandris Group), Panamanian flag.
1996: Laid-up at Perama Bay; plans to reactivate the ship never materialized.
2001: Scrapped at Alang, India.

8

Cogedar Line

Aurelia

Service: Charter summer season New York–Le Havre –Southampton. Otherwise: Bremerhaven–Rotterdam–Southampton–Port Said–Suez–Aden–Fremantle–Melbourne–Sydney.
Particulars: 10,480 gross tons; 487 × 60 × 21 feet.
Builders: Blohm & Voss A/G, Hamburg, Germany, 1939.
Machinery: MAN type diesels; single screw; service speed 17 knots.
Capacity: 1,124 all-tourist class passengers.

1939–47: Known as *Huascaran*, Hamburg America Line; combination passenger-cargo ship.
1947–54: Sailed as *Beaverbrae* for Canadian Pacific Steamships (qv).
November 1, 1954: Purchased by Cogedar Line, Italian flag; renamed *Aurelia*.
November 1954–May 1955: Extensively rebuilt at Monfalcone; capacity increased from 773 to 1,124 passengers.
May 1955: Commenced Australian migrant service from Genoa and Naples.
1958–59: Original diesel-electric engines replaced by new MAN diesels; tonnage relisted from 10,022 to 10,480.
1959: Commenced extended Australian sailings from Bremerhaven, Rotterdam, and Southampton; also first cruise from Sydney to South Pacific ports.
June 1960: Began summer charters to Council of Student Travel; Southampton–Le Havre–New York.
September 23, 1968: Final roundtrip sailing from Rotterdam and Southampton to Australia. Extensive refit followed; 470 one-class cruise passengers only.
January 12, 1969: Commenced Southampton–Canary Islands cruise service; unsuccessful.
May 1970: Sold to International Cruises S/A (Chandris Group), Greek flag; renamed *Romanza* for Mediterranean and Black Sea cruising.
1977: Changed to Panamanian registry.
1979: Transferred to Amadones Romanza S/A (Chandris Group).
October 17, 1979: Ran aground in the Aegean Sea during a cruise; heavily damaged but later refloated and then repaired.
1983: Passenger capacity relisted as 707.
1991: Sold to Columbia Ship Management, Cypriot flag; renamed *Romantica*. Eastern Mediterranean cruising for Ambassador Leisure Cruises.
August 1, 1997: Destroyed by fire in the Eastern Mediterranean; later towed to Alexandria.
April 1998: Scrapped at Alexandria.

The former *Aurelia* burned out and a complete loss in this view from 1997. (*Peter Knego collection*)

9

Companhia Colonial

Vera Cruz

Service: 1957–58: Lisbon–Madeira–Tenerife–La Guaira–Curaçao–Havana–Port Everglades–Tenerife–Madeira–Lisbon.
Particulars: 21,765 gross tons; 610 × 76 × 27 feet.
Builders: John Cockerill Shipyard S/A, Hoboken, Belgium, 1952.
Machinery: Steam turbines; twin screw; service speed 20 knots.
Capacity: 148 first class, 250 cabin class, and 844 third class.

June 2, 1951: Launched.
February 1952: Completed; Portugal–Brazil service: Lisbon–Funchal–Sao Vicente–Recife–Salvador–Rio de Janeiro–Santos.
1957–58: Lisbon–Caribbean–Florida voyages.
1960: Began Lisbon–Africa service mostly.
January 1972: Laid-up at Lisbon.
March 4, 1973: Departed Lisbon for Kaohsiung to be scrapped.
April 19, 1973: Arrived at Kaohsiung.

Santa Maria

Service: Same ports as *Vera Cruz*, but after 1959, Havana replaced by San Juan.
Particulars: 20,906 gross tons; 609 × 76 × 27 feet.
Builders: John Cockerill Shipyard S/A, Hoboken, Belgium, 1953.
Machinery: Steam turbines; twin screw; service speed 20 knots.
Capacity: 156 first class, 226 cabin class, and 696 third class.

September 20, 1952: Launched.
September 1953: Maiden voyage from Lisbon to Santos.
1953–56: Lisbon–South America service.
December 1956: Began service to the Caribbean and Florida.
January 22, 1961: Hijacked in the Caribbean by Portuguese political rebels; rerouted to Brazil.
February 2, 1961: Arrived at Recife; passengers freed; rebels later surrendered and ship returned to owners.
April 11, 1973: Arrived at Lisbon after final voyage from Port Everglades.
July 19, 1973: Arrived at Kaohsiung for scrapping.

Bound for Lisbon: The *Santa Maria* prepares to sail from Port Everglades. (*ALF collection*)

10

Costa Line

Federico C

Service: 1966–70: Naples, Genoa, Cannes, Barcelona, Lisbon, and Funchal to Port Everglades; winter cruises to the Caribbean from Port Everglades.
Particulars: 20,416 gross tons; 606 × 79 × 27 feet.
Builders: Ansaldo Shipyard, Genoa, Italy, 1958.
Machinery: Steam turbines; twin screw; service speed 21 knots.
Capacity: 243 first class, 300 cabin class, and 736 tourist class.
Notes: First new passenger ship built for Costa Line.

March 31, 1957: Launched.
March 22, 1958: Left Genoa on maiden voyage to Rio de Janeiro, Santos, Montevideo, and Buenos Aires. Thereafter Italy–South America service.
April 1966: Commenced service Mediterranean–Florida.
1968: Accommodation restyled as 186 first class and 1,450 tourist class.
1970: Cruising only.
December 8, 1973: Grounded off Port Everglades; later refloated.
1976–77: Given $2 million refit upgrading accommodation.
1977: Winter cruising to the Caribbean from Port Everglades; Mediterranean cruising in summer from Genoa.
December 1983: Sold to Premier Cruise Lines, Panamanian flag; renamed *Royale*; cruising from U.S. East Coast ports.
February 1984: Commenced cruising from Port Canaveral.
1997: Renamed *Sea Breeze I.*
September 2000: Sought for debts following collapse of Premier Cruises.
December 17, 2000: Sank off Virginia when sailing without passengers from Halifax to Charleston.

Completed in 1958, the *Federico C* was the first brand new liner for Costa Line. (*ALF collection*)

11

Cunard Line

Aquitania

Service: Post-war austerity service: Southampton–Halifax.
Particulars: 45,647 gross tons; 901 × 97 × 36 feet.
Builders: John Brown & Co. Ltd., Clydebank, Scotland, 1914.
Machinery: Steam triple-expansion turbines; quadruple screw; service speed 23½ knots.
Capacity: Approximately 2,200 in a single austerity class.
Notes: One of the world's great liners; last four-funnel passenger ship.

December 1910: Designed to sail with *Mauretania* and *Lusitania* on Liverpool–New York express service.
April 21, 1913: Launched.
May 1914: Sea trials.
August 1914: Converted to armed merchant cruise for war service.
1915: Used as hospital ship.
1916–18: Used as troopship.
June 1919: Returned to service; Southampton–New York; 618 first class, 614 second class, and 1,998 third class.
December 1919: Converted from coal to oil.
1939–48: Trooping.
1948–49: Migrant, etc. service between Southampton and Halifax; twelve voyages in 1948, thirteen in 1949.
December 1, 1949: Completed final voyage at Southampton: 443 sailings, thirty-five years of service, 3 million steaming miles, and carried 1.2 million passengers.
1950: Scrapped at Faslane, Scotland.

Scythia

Service: 1950–57: Mostly sailings between London or Southampton, Le Havre, and Quebec City; occasional sailings to New York via Halifax.
Particulars: 19,930 gross tons; 624 × 73 feet.
Builders: Vickers-Armstrong Shipbuilders Ltd., Barrow-in-Furness, England 1920.
Machinery: Steam turbines; geared to twin screw; service speed 16 knots.
Capacity: 248 first class and 630 tourist class.

March 22, 1920: Launched; completed at L'Orient, France, owing to British shipbuilding strikes.
August 20, 1921: Departed from Liverpool on maiden voyage to New York; 350 first class, 350 second class and 1,500 third class.
1939–48: Government trooping.
November 23, 1942: Damaged in bombing at Algiers; towed to Gibraltar; and later sent to New York for repairs.
1948: Made ten roundtrip voyages Cuxhaven (Hamburg)–Le Havre–Quebec or Halifax–New York.
November 1949: Commenced major refit for restoration to peacetime service.
August 17, 1950: Post-war maiden voyage from Liverpool to Quebec City; thereafter from London or Southampton via Le Havre.
June 5, 1952: Collision in St Lawrence River with collier *Wabana*.
October 1957: Final Cunard crossing: Liverpool–Cobh–New York.
October–November 1957: Two trooping voyages for Canadian Government; Quebec City–Rotterdam.
December 22, 1957: Arrived at Southampton; laid-up.
January 1958: Sailed for Inverkeithing, Scotland to be scrapped.

Samaria

Service: 1950–57: Mostly sailings between London or Southampton, Le Havre, and Quebec City; winter sailings to Halifax.
Particulars: 19,848 gross tons; 624 × 73 feet.

Above left: Awaiting a final voyage to the scrappers, the veteran *Aquitania* waits at Southampton in this late 1949 photo. (*Richard Weiss collection*)

Above right: Between Crossings: The *Scythia* at Pier 92, New York. (*Cunard*)

Right: The *Scythia* loads vintage autos at Liverpool. (*Cunard*)

Builders: Vickers-Armstrong Shipbuilders Ltd., Barrow-in-Furness, England 1921.
Machinery: Steam turbines; geared to twin screw; service speed 16 knots.
Capacity: 250 first class and 650 tourist class.

November 27, 1920: Launched.
April 19, 1922: Departed from Liverpool on maiden voyage to Boston; 350 first class, 350 second class, and 1,500 third class.
1926: Transferred to Liverpool–New York service; usually via Boston.
1939–48: Government trooping.
September 1948: Hamburg–Le Havre–Quebec City or Halifax austerity service.
1950: London–Quebec City austerity service.
October 1950: Began major refit; fully restored; 250 first class and 650 tourist class.
June 1951: Commenced Cunard liner service: Southampton–Le Havre–Quebec City.
June 15, 1953: Represented Cunard at Coronation Review at Spithead.
November 1955: Final Cunard sailing: Quebec City–Southampton.
January 1956: Sold to scrappers at Inverkeithing, Scotland.

Franconia (1923)

Service: Mostly sailings between Liverpool and Quebec City; and occasional sailings from Liverpool and Cobh to New York via Halifax.

Particulars: 20,341 gross tons; 623 × 73 feet.
Builders: John Brown & Co. Ltd., Clydebank, Scotland, 1923.
Machinery: Steam turbines; geared to twin screw; service speed 16 knots.
Capacity: 250 first class and 600 tourist class.

October 21, 1922: Launched.
June 23, 1923: Departed from Liverpool on maiden voyage to New York.
1929–39: Liverpool or London–New York service; considerable cruising.
1930–31: Major refit; made more suitable for cruising.
September 1939: Began wartime trooping.
October 5, 1939 Oct: Collided with Royal Mail Lines' *Alcantara* in the Mediterranean; damaged and later repaired.
June 16, 1940: Damaged by Nazi bombers off France; later repaired.
February 1945: Used as Winston Churchill's floating headquarters and accommodation ship during Yalta Conference.
1948–49: Major refit and restoration.
June 2, 1949: Departed Liverpool on post-war maiden sailing to Quebec City.
November 1956: Final Cunard sailing from New York to Liverpool.
December 1956: Sailed from Liverpool to Inverkeithing for scrapping.

Ascania (1925)

Service: Liverpool to Quebec City and Montreal during summer season; to Halifax and occasionally New York during winter.
Particulars: 14,440 gross tons; 538 × 65 feet.
Builders: Armstrong-Whitworth Co. Ltd., Newcastle-upon-Tyne, England, 1925.
Machinery: Steam turbines; geared to twin screw; service speed 15 knots.
Capacity: 198 first class and 498 tourist class.

December 20, 1923: Launched.
May 22, 1925: Departed from London on maiden voyage via Southampton to Quebec City and Montreal; 500 cabin class and 1,200 third class; also occasional cruising.
July 2, 1938: Aground in the St. Lawrence River.
1939–48: Trooping.
1949: Major refit and restoration.
April 21, 1950: Departed Liverpool on first post-war sailing to Quebec City and Montreal.
November 1956: Final Cunard sailing: Montreal–Southampton.
December 1956: Trooping voyage for British Ministry of Transport to Port Said.
December 30, 1956: Departed from Southampton for Newport, Monmouthshire for scrapping.

Britannic

Service: Liverpool–Cobh–New York. Annual long winter cruise from New York to the Mediterranean and Black Sea.
Particulars: 27,666 gross tons; 712 × 82 feet.
Builders: Harland & Wolff Ltd., Belfast, Northern Ireland, 1930.
Machinery: B&W type diesels; geared to twin screw; service speed 18 knots.
Capacity: 429 first class and 564 tourist class.
Notes: The last liner to wear White Star Line colors.

Rainy Afternoon: The *Ascania* loading at New York. (*Gillespie-Faber collection*)

The stately *Britannic* arrives at Boston. (*Anton Logvinenko*)

August 6, 1929: Launched for White Star Line, British flag.
June 28, 1930: Departed from Liverpool on maiden voyage to New York; 504 cabin class, 551 tourist class and 498 third class.
April 1934: Acquired as part of Cunard-White Star merger.
1935: Transferred to London–Le Havre–Southampton–New York service.
1939–47: Wartime trooping.
1947–48: Major refit and restoration; tonnage revised from 26,943 to 27,666; capacity reduced to 993 passengers.
May 22, 1948: Departed Liverpool on first post-war crossing to New York via Cobh.
June 1960: Broken crankshaft; idle at Pier 90, New York; extended major repairs.
December 1960: Sold for scrapping at Inverkeithing, Scotland.

Georgic

Service: 1950–54: Cunard charter summer sailings between Liverpool or Southampton, Le Havre and Cobh to Halifax (westbound only) and New York; occasional sailings to New York via Halifax. Otherwise migrant service to Australia and use by British Government to carry troops.
Particulars: 27,469 gross tons; 711 × 82 feet.
Builders: Harland & Wolff Ltd., Belfast Northern Ireland, 1932.
Machinery: B&W type diesels; geared to twin screw; service speed 18 knots.
Capacity: 1,962 one-class passengers.
November 12, 1931: Launched for White Star Line, British flag.
June 1932: Entered Liverpool–New York service.
April 1934: Transferred in Cunard-White Star merger.
1935: Transferred to London–Le Havre–Southampton–New York service; considerable cruising.
September 1939: Became troopship for war duties.
September 14, 1941: Set afire by Nazi bombers at Port Tewfik, Egypt; badly damaged and burnt out.
October 27, 1941: Salvaged.
December 29, 1941: Began tow to Port Sudan.
March 31, 1942: Reached Karachi.
December 1942: At Bombay; further repairs.
January 1943: Long tow from Bombay to Liverpool via South Africa; then major rebuilding at Belfast; forward funnel and mainmast removed; sold to British Ministry of Transport.
December 1944: Resumed trooping service after three-year disruption.
1948: Converted to one-class migrant ship.
January 1949: Commenced Liverpool–Suez–Sydney sailings; also periodic trooping.
1950–54: Chartered to Cunard for summer season crossings.
October 1954: Final Cunard sailing: New York–Halifax–Southampton.
1955: Final season on Australian migrant run.
February 1956: Scrapped at Faslane.

Left: The post-war *Georgic* with only one funnel. (*Cunard Line*)

Below: Preparing to Sail: The *Queen Mary* at Southampton. (*Mick Lindsay collection*)

Queen Mary

Service: Southampton–Cherbourg–New York.
Particulars: 81,237 gross tons; 1,019 × 119 × 39 feet.
Builders: John Brown & Co. Ltd., Clydebank, Scotland, 1930–36.
Machinery: Steam turbines; geared to quadruple screw; service speed 28½ knots.
Capacity: 711 first class, 707 cabin class, and 577 tourist class.
Notes: World's fastest liner 1938–1952; first major Cunarder to dispense with traditional "ia" ending in name; last three-funnel passenger liner.

December 27, 1930: Keel laid.
December 1931–April 1934: Construction halted owing to Depression.
September 26, 1934: Launched by HM Queen Mary.
May 27, 1936: Departed from Southampton on maiden voyage to New York.
August 1936: Captured Blue Riband by averaging over 30 knots from French *Normandie*.
March 1937: Riband recaptured by *Normandie* at 30.9 knots.
August 1938: *Queen Mary* firmly retook Riband from the *Normandie* at 31.6 knots; record stood until taken by the *United States* in July 1952.
September 1939: Laid-up at Pier 90, New York for safety.
March 1, 1940: Commissioned as a troopship at New York; later sailed New York–Cape Town–Sydney.
May 5, 1940: Sailed from Sydney as a troopship.
October 2, 1942: Rammed and sank British cruiser *Curacoa* off Northern Ireland; 338 casualties from warship.
September 1946: Decommissioned from war duties at Southampton; later major refit and restoration at Clydebank.
July 31, 1947: Sailed from Southampton on first post-war liner voyage to New York.
1958: Stabilizers added during winter overhaul.
December 1963: First cruise: Southampton–Las Palmas.
March 1967: Rumor that Australian syndicate planned to buy ship for conversion to migrant ship; also rumors that ship might become school at Brooklyn and casino at Gibraltar.
1967: Loss of some $2 million in operations.
September 22, 1967: Final sailing: New York–Cherbourg–Southampton.
October 1967: Sold to City of Long Beach, California, for over $3 million.
October 31, 1967: Left Southampton for last time; farewell cruise around South America to Long Beach; extensive, three-year refit at Long Beach Naval Shipyard costing over $40 million.
February 28, 1971: Moved to permanent berth at Long Beach.

One of the most popular and successful liners of all time, the *Queen Mary* makes a midday arrival along the Hudson River. (*ALF collection*)

The classic *Queen Mary* meets the newer, larger *Queen Mary 2* at Long Beach in a scene from January 2006. (*Cunard*)

May 8, 1971: Opened to the public as museum, convention center, collection of shops and restaurants and hotel. Total renovations costing in excess of $60 million.
1971–74: Managed by Pacific Southwest Airlines.
1974–80: Management by Hyatt Hotels Inc.
December 1978: Less than successful; rumored to be for sale.
November 1980: Management taken over by the Wrather Port Properties Corp.
1988: Management transferred to Disney Corp.
1993: Plan to take ship to Japan in a large floating dock, then put on display in Tokyo Bay and also given major refurbishing; never materialized. Management changed to RMS Foundation Inc.
January 2006: First meeting with *Queen Mary 2.*
2009: Management changed to Delaware North Companies.
2011: Management changed to Evolution Hospitality Inc.
2014: Celebrations for eightieth anniversary of launching of the ship.
2016: Management changed to Urban Commons Inc.
2017: Found to be in need of substantial repairs and renewal; considerable corrosion.
December 2017: Fiftieth anniversary of first arrival in California.

Stratheden

Service: Cunard charter for four sailings: Southampton–Le Havre–New York.
Particulars: 23,732 gross tons; 664 × 82 × 30 feet.
Builders: Vickers-Armstrong Shipbuilders Ltd., Barrow-in-Furness, England, 1937.
Machinery: Steam turbines; geared to twin screw; service speed 19 knots.
Capacity: 527 first class and 453 tourist class.
Notes: First P&O liner to visit New York in peacetime.

June 10, 1937: Launched by Duchess of Buccleuch & Queensferry; P&O Lines flagship.
December 1937: Maiden voyage from London to Australia via Suez.
1938–39: Australian service and Mediterranean cruises.
1939–46: Trooping.
1946–47: Refit and restoration.
June 1947: First post-war sailing from London to Sydney.
June 1950: Began four Cunard voyages to New York.
1961: Accommodation restyled for 1,200 one-class passengers.

1964: Sold to John S. Latsis Line, Greek flag; renamed *Henrietta Latsi*; used as a pilgrim ship in Mediterranean, African, and Middle Eastern waters.
1966: Renamed *Marianna Latsi.*
May 19, 1969: Arrived at La Spezia for scrapping.

Mauretania

Service: Southampton–Le Havre–Cobh–New York; winter cruising from New York to the Caribbean.
Particulars: 35,655 gross tons; 772 × 89 × 30 feet.
Builders: Cammell Laird & Co. Ltd., Birkenhead, England, 1939.
Machinery: Steam turbines; geared to twin screw; service speed 23 knots.
Capacity: 470 first class, 370 cabin class, and 300 tourist class.

July 28, 1938: Launched.
June 17, 1939: Departed from Liverpool on maiden voyage to New York; then Southampton–Le Havre–New York service.
December 1939: Laid-up at New York for safety.
March 6, 1940: Sailed New York–Sydney; then converted for trooping.
1940–46: Wartime trooping.
January 8, 1944: Collided with American tanker *Hat Creek* outside New York harbor.
September 2, 1946: Decommissioned from war duties; later restored at Liverpool.
June 10, 1947: Left Southampton on first post-war sailing to New York.
1957: Made fully air-conditioned.
December 1962: Repainted in green; used mostly for cruising.
1963: Experimental season on Naples–Genoa–Cannes–Gibraltar–New York service; highly unsuccessful.
October 1964: Chartered to Regent Refining Co. Ltd. to carry guests to opening of new refinery at Milford Haven; guests included HM Queen Elizabeth the Queen Mother.
November 23, 1965: Arrived at Firth of Forth; scrapped at Inverkeithing.

Queen Elizabeth

Service: Southampton–Cherbourg–New York service.
Particulars: 83,673 gross tons; 1,031 × 119 × 39 feet.
Builders: John Brown & Co. Ltd., Clydebank, Scotland, 1936–40.

The handsome *Mauretania* arrives off Lower Manhattan. (*ALF collection*)

Repainted in all-green, the *Mauretania* is seen from the upper decks of the *Queen Mary* at Southampton. (*Mick Lindsay collection*)

Machinery: Steam turbines; geared to quadruple screw; service speed 28½ knots.
Capacity: 823 first class, 662 cabin class, and 798 tourist class.
Notes: Largest passenger liner of her time.

December 1936: Keel laid.
September 27, 1938: Launched by HM Queen Elizabeth (later HM Queen Elizabeth the Queen Mother).
February 26, 1940: Darted for safety directly from Clydebank to New York; arriving on March 7.
November 1940: Sailed from New York to begin war duties.
1940–46: Wartime trooping: Total 800,000 passengers and 500,000 miles steamed.
March 6, 1946: First Cunarder released from war service.

Above left: The mighty *Queen Elizabeth* departs from Southampton's Ocean Terminal. (*Mick Lindsay collection*)

Above right: Stern View: The *Queen Elizabeth* with the *Athlone Castle* just beyond at Southampton's Western Docks. (*Mick Lindsay collection*)

Right: Being repainted in all white at Hong Kong, the renamed *Seawise University* is seen in this 1971 photo. (*Tim Noble collection*)

March 8, 1946: Fire at Southampton; later major refit and restoration.
October 16, 1946: Departed from Southampton on maiden voyage to New York.
1947: Aground off Bramble Bank for twenty-four hours.
December 4, 1952: Collided with tug in New York; minor damage.
October 1954: Carried HM Queen Elizabeth the Queen Mother as a passenger from Southampton to New York.
1954–55: During winter overhaul fitted with stabilizers.
August 1959: Collision outside New York harbor with United States Lines' freighter *American Hunter*.
December 1960: Refit.
December 1965: Began three-month, £1.5 million refit at Firth of Forth Graving dock. Full air-conditioning and lido deck installed; improvements to passenger and crew accommodation so as to ensure extended operation until 1975; tonnage relisted as 82,998.
1967: Loss of $2 million in operations.
November 8, 1968: Final Cunard sailing: Southampton–Las Palmas–Gibraltar–Southampton cruise. Completed record of 907 Atlantic crossings, 3,470,000 miles, and 2,300,000 passengers.
November 1968: Sold to American financial interests.
November 29, 1968: Departed from Southampton for Port Everglades, arriving there on December 8. Later idle at Port Everglades; legal problems and later bankruptcy.
July 19, 1969: Sold to the Queen Ltd., U.S. flag, for $8½ million; remained idle at Port Everglades.
July 1970: Bankrupt again.
September 9–10, 1970: Auctioned off for $3.2 million to Seawise Foundations Ltd. (C. Y. Tung Group), Bahamian flag; renamed *Seawise University*.
February 10, 1971: Departed Port Everglades for Hong Kong via Cape Town; mechanical troubles.

Grotesquely canted over and fire gutted, the once glorious *Queen Elizabeth* has met a ruinous end. (*Des Kirkpatrick collection*)

1971: Refitted at Hong Kong as floating university-cruise ship.
January 8–9, 1972: Destroyed by fire at Hong Kong; burnt out and capsized.
January 13, 1972: Last fire extinguished. Later scrapped on the spot.

Media

Service: Liverpool–New York; occasionally via Bermuda or Norfolk.
Particulars: 13,345 gross tons; 531 × 70 × 30 feet.
Builders: John Brown & Co. Ltd. Clydebank, Scotland, 1947.
Machinery: Steam turbines; geared to twin screw; service speed 18 knots.
Capacity: 250 first class only.
Notes: First post-war passenger ship to be completed; first Atlantic passenger ship to have stabilizers.

December 12, 1946: Launched.
August 1947: Maiden voyage: Liverpool–New York.
January 1953: During winter overhaul fitted with stabilizers.
September 1961: Sold to Cogedar Line, Italian flag; renamed *Flavia*; thoroughly rebuilt at Genoa for Australian migrant trade; 1,320 all-tourist class passengers; lengthened to 557 feet.
December 1962: First sailing to Australia from Bremerhaven, Rotterdam, Southampton, and Genoa.
1968: Transferred to Costa Line, also Italian flag; refitted for 800 one-class cruise passengers.
December 21, 1968: First sailing from Miami to Nassau.
1977–78: Mediterranean cruise service.
December 1978: Resumed Miami–Nassau cruise service.
1982: Sold to Flavian Shipping S/A, Panamanian flag; renamed *Flavian*.
October 25, 1982: Laid-up at Hong Kong.
1988: Sold to Lavia Shipping S/A, Panamanian flag; renamed *Lavia*; planned reuse as a cruise ship never materialized.
January 7, 1989: Destroyed by fire at Hong Kong; towed to outer harbor; capsized; later refloated.
June 19, 1989: Arrived under tow at Kaohsiung to be scrapped.

Parthia

Service: Liverpool–New York (see *Media*).
Particulars: 13,362 gross tons; 531 × 70 × 30 feet.
Builders: Harland & Wolff Ltd., Belfast, Norther Ireland, 1948.
Machinery: Steam turbines; geared to twin screw; service speed 18 knots.
Capacity: 250 first class only.
February 25, 1947: Launched.
April 10, 1948: Left Liverpool on maiden voyage to New York.
September 1961: Final Cunard voyage.
November 1961: Sold to New Zealand Shipping Co., also British flag; renamed *Remuera* (qv).

The *Parthia* arrives in New York on her maiden voyage in April 1948. (*Gillespie-Faber collection*)

Caronia

Service: Occasional Southampton–Le Havre–New York sailings; annual westbound winter voyage via Caribbean ports, Nassau and Bermuda. Mostly long cruises from New York.
Particulars: 34,172 gross tons; 715 × 91 × 31 feet.
Builders: John Brown & Co. Ltd., Clydebank, Scotland, 1948.
Machinery: Steam turbines; geared to twin screw; service speed 22 knots.
Capacity: 581 first class and 351 cabin class.
Notes: In 1948, the largest liner yet built with luxury cruising in mind; also Britain's largest post-war liner and largest liner with a single funnel.

October 30, 1947: Launched by HRH Princess Elizabeth (later HM Queen Elizabeth II).
January 4, 1949: Left Southampton on maiden voyage to New York.
April 14, 1958: Rammed lighthouse and pushing it into the sea at Yokohama; ship damaged and later repaired at Yokohama.
October 1965: Three-month refit begun at Harland & Wolff, Belfast.
November 1967: Laid-up at Southampton; offered for sale.
January 1968: Intended sale to Dumas Turist, Yugoslavia, for use as floating hotel; on the Dalmatian coast; never materialized.
May 24, 1968: Sold to Star Line, Panamanian flag; owners later relisted as Universal Line S/A, also Panamanian flag; renamed *Columbia* then *Caribia*.
July 26, 1968: Transferred to new owners at Southampton.
September 1968: Commenced refit at Piraeus and later at Naples.
February 14, 1969: Departure from New York on maiden Caribbean cruise as *Caribia*.
March 5, 1969: Engine room explosion in the Caribbean; towed to New York for repairs.
March 25, 1969: Repairs suspended; laid-up at New York. Plans to reactivate ship never materialized.
February 1974: Fittings auctioned-off at Pier 56, New York; sold to Taiwanese shipbreakers.
April 27, 1974: Left New York under tow for Taiwan for scrapping.
July 11, 1974: At Honolulu with flooding problems.
August 12, 1974: Put into Guam in heavy weather; towlines snapped; ship struck breakwater and broke in three sections; later scrapped on the spot.

Mediterranean Cruising: The luxurious *Caronia* at Malta. (*ALF collection*)

A New Quartet: The handsome *Saxonia* at Quebec City. (*ALF collection*)

Saxonia/Carmania

Service: Southampton–Le Havre–occasionally Cobh–Quebec City–Montreal between April and December; to Halifax and New York December to April.
Particulars: 21,367 gross tons; 608 × 80 × 28 feet.
Builders: John Brown & Co. Ltd., Clydebank, Scotland, 1954.
Machinery: Steam turbines; geared to twin screw; service speed 19½ knots.
Capacity: 125 first class and 800 tourist class.

February 17, 1954: Launched by Lady Churchill as *Saxonia*.
September 2, 1954: Left Liverpool on maiden voyage to Montreal; later switched to Southampton service.
1962–63: Major refit at Clydebank: Repainted in green; given full air-conditioning, lido deck and improved passenger

The smart looking *Carmania* (ex-*Saxonia*) at Southampton. (*Mick Lindsay collection*)

accommodation; berthing restyled for 117 first class and 764 tourist class; renamed *Carmania*.
April 1963: Commenced Rotterdam-Southampton–Montreal service; winter cruising from Port Everglades to the Caribbean.
February 1967: Hull repainted in white.
January 12, 1969: Aground on San Salvador Island, the Bahamas; passengers taken ashore; refloated on January 17. Later taken to Newport News Shipyard in Virginia for repairs.
May 14, 1969: Collided with Soviet tanker *Frunze* off Gibraltar.
April 1971: Rumored sale to Chandris Lines; never materialized.
December 1971: Laid-up; offered for sale. Sale to Carnival Cruise Lines never materialized.
May 15, 1972: Continued in lay-up but transferred to River Fal, Cornwall.
May 1972: Later sale to Toyo Yusen KK, Japanese flag, for Far East cruising; never materialized.
August 1973: Sold to Nikreis Maritime Corp as agents for Black Sea Steamship Co., U.S.S.R. flag; renamed *Leonid Sobinov.* Refitted and later chartered to CTC Lines for cruising and U.K.–Australia sailings.
June 1980: Being used by Cuban Government to transport troops between Havana and the Middle East and Africa.
1983: Tonnage relisted as 21,846.
1989: Repairs at Piraeus with machinery troubles.
1990: Owners changed to Transblasco Four Shipping Co. Ltd., Maltese flag.
1991: Declining condition.
1995: Laid-up.
April 1999: Arrived at Alang, India, to be scrapped.

Ivernia/Franconia (1955)

Service: Southampton–Le Havre–occasionally Cobh–Quebec City–Montreal between April and December; to Halifax and New York December to April.
Particulars: 21,717 gross tons; 608 × 80 × 28 feet.
Builders: John Brown & Co. Ltd., Clydebank, Scotland, 1955.
Machinery: Steam turbines; geared to twin screw; service speed 19½ knots.
Capacity: 125 first class and 800 tourist class.

December 1, 1954: Launched.
July 1, 1955: Departed Greenock on maiden voyage to Montreal; thereafter based at Southampton.
1962–63: Major refit at Clydebank: Repainted in green; given full air-conditioning, lido deck and improved passenger accommodation; berthing restyled for 119 first class and 728 tourist class; tonnage relisted as 22,637; renamed *Franconia.*
July 1963: Commenced Rotterdam–Southampton–Montreal service; winter cruising from New York to the Caribbean.
February 1967: Hull repainted in white.
April 1967: Began weekly New York–Bermuda cruise service.
December 1970: Engine trouble during Caribbean cruise.
April 1971: Rumored sale to Chandris Lines for rebuilding for U.K.–Australia service; never materialized.
December 1971: Laid-up; offered for sale. Sale to Carnival Cruise Lines never materialized.
May 15, 1972 May: Continued in lay-up but transferred to River Fal, Cornwall.
May 1972: Later sale to Toyo Yusen KK, Japanese flag, for Far East cruising; never materialized.
August 1973: Sold to Nikreis Maritime Corp as agents for Black Sea Steamship Co., U.S.S.R. flag; renamed *Fyodor*

The restyled *Franconia*, the former *Ivernia*, prepares to depart. (*ALF collection*).

Sisters Together: The *Leonid Sobinov* and *Fyodor Shalyapin* together at Malta. (*Michael Cassar*)

Shalyapin. Refitted and later chartered to CTC Lines for cruising and U.K.–Australia sailings.
November 20, 1973: First sailing Southampton-Suez-Sydney for CTC Lines.
June 1980: Being used by Cuban Government to transport troops between Havana and the Middle East and Africa.
1990: Owners changed to Transblasco Four Shipping Co. Ltd., Maltese flag.
1992: Transferred to Odessa Cruise Co., Maltese flag. Hereafter declining condition and engine troubles.
February 3, 1996: Laid-up at Ilyichevsk.
November 2003: Sold to Indian scrappers; renamed *Salona*; later towed to Alang for scrapping.
February 11, 2004: Arrived Alang for demolition.

Carinthia

Service: Liverpool–Greenock–Quebec City–Montreal service between April and December; to Halifax and New York December to April.
Particulars: 21,947 gross tons; 608 × 80 × 28 feet.
Builders: John Brown & Co. Ltd., Clydebank, Scotland, 1956.
Machinery: Steam turbines; geared to twin screw; service speed 19½ knots.
Capacity: 154 first class and 714 tourist class.

December 23, 1954: Laid down.
December 14, 1955: Launched by HRH Princess Margaret.
June 27, 1956: Left Liverpool on maiden voyage to Montreal.
February 1967: Hull repainted in white.
October 13, 1967: Departed from Liverpool on final Cunard crossing to Montreal; later laid-up at Southampton.
May 4, 1968: Sold to Sitmar Line, Liberian flag; renamed *Fairland* then changed to *Fairsea*. Intended for U.K.–Australia and around-the-world services.
February 21, 1970: Arrived at Trieste; rebuilt for year-round cruising instead; 910 one-class passengers; tonnage later relisted as 21,916.
December 17, 1971: Entered service for Sitmar Cruises: San Francisco–Los Angeles–Mexico cruises (summers San Francisco–Alaska–British Columbia).
September 1976: Damaged while in dry-dock at Alameda, California.
1984: Changed to 906 passengers.
July 1988: Sold to P&O Group; renamed *Fair Princess* for use by Princess Cruises.
1997: Based in Sydney for South Pacific cruising.
2000: Sold to Hong Kong buyers, Liberian flag; renamed *China Sea Discovery*; gambling cruises from Hong Kong.
December 2002: Gambling cruises from Keelung; later from Kaohsiung.
2003: Unsuccessful; later laid-up at Kaohsiung.
November 22, 2005: Arrived at Alang for scrapping.

Sylvania

Service: Liverpool–Montreal (see *Carinthia*).
Particulars: 21,989 gross tons; 608 × 80 × 28 feet.
Builders: John Brown & Co. Ltd., Clydebank, Scotland, 1957.
Machinery: Steam turbines; geared to twin screw; service speed 19½ knots.
Capacity: 154 first class and 724 tourist class.

November 22, 1956: Launched.
June 5, 1957: Departed Liverpool on maiden voyage to Montreal.
April 1961: Transferred to year-round Liverpool–Cobh–New York service.
September 1964: Refitted.
October 1964: Twenty-seven-day Mediterranean cruise: first Cunard cruise from Liverpool since 1939.
November 24, 1966: Terminated Cunard's New York–Liverpool service.
December 1966: Repainted in white for further cruising.
May 1968: Laid-up at Southampton; offered for sale.
July 5, 1968: Sold to Sitmar Line, Liberian flag; renamed *Fairwind.*
January 6, 1970: Left Southampton under tow for Trieste; major refit afterward for fulltime cruising.
July 1, 1972: Entered cruise service: San Francisco–Los Angeles–Mexico; later transferred to Port Everglades–Caribbean cruising.
November 29, 1975: Engine room fire in the Caribbean; later repaired.
1988: Briefly repainted in new Sitmar colors.
September 1988: Sold to P&O Group; renamed *Dawn Princess* for use by Princess Cruises.
1993: Sold to Bahamian-flag buyers and chartered to Phoenix Reisen; renamed *Albatros.* Worldwide cruising, but subsequent frequent engine troubles.
December 2003: Laid-up with mechanical problems.
January 2004: Renamed *Genoa*; towed to Alang; scrapped.

Queen Elizabeth 2

Service: May–December: Southampton–Cherbourg–New York. Considerable cruising.
Particulars: 65,863 gross tons; 963 × 105 × 32 feet.
Builders: Upper Clyde Shipbuilders Ltd. (formerly John Brown & Co. Ltd.), Clydebank, Scotland, 1930–36.
Machinery: Steam turbines; geared to quadruple screw; service speed 28½ knots.
Capacity: 564 first class and 1,441 tourist class.
Notes: Longest lasting, most traveled and overall most successful Atlantic super liner ever built.

June 5, 1965: Keel laid.
September 20, 1967: Launched by HM Queen Elizabeth II.
November 26, 1968: Left Greenock for sea trials; serious turbine troubles and other defects; Cunard refused delivery from shipbuilder.
January 2, 1969: Docked at Southampton; Cunard still refused acceptance.
January 1969: Intended maiden voyage canceled.
March 1969: Fresh trials, averaging 32.66 knots.
April 18, 1969: Finally delivered to Cunard; delays cost £3 million.
May 2, 1969: Departed Southampton on maiden voyage to New York.
January 9, 1971: Rescued survivors from the burning French liner *Antilles* off Mustique in the Caribbean.
1972: Capacity restyled as 604 first class and 1,223 tourist class; 1,740 one-class for cruising.
April 1, 1974: Immobilized by turbines troubles while at sea and some 280 miles southwest of Bermuda.
April 3, 1974: 1,630 passengers transferred at sea to nearby cruise ship *Sea Venture.*
April 7, 1974: Towed to Bermuda.
December 1975: Damaged hull on coral reef at Nassau.
July 23, 1976: Engine room fire while at sea; forced to return to Southampton.
1976: Capacity relisted as 1,820 one-class for all sailings.
December 1977: New suites added; tonnage relisted as 67,107 gross tons.
September 1978: Damaged in North Atlantic storm.
December 1979: Extensive refit at Bayonne, New Jersey shipyard.
May 12, 1982: Requisitioned as a troopship for Falklands War.
June 1982: Returned to Southampton; later restored.
August 14, 1982: Resumed commercial sailings following refit: Cunard funnel colors added and hull coloring changed to light grey.
1983: Hull coloring reverted to dark coloring.
October 27, 1986: Arrived at Bremerhaven to be extensively refitted and re-engined with diesel-electric machinery; capacity relisted as 1,870 passengers.
April 1987: Resumed sailing.
March 30–June 9, 1989: Used as hotel ship at Yokohama in connection with port's 150th anniversary.
August 8, 1992: Aground off Martha's Vineyard; damages.
October 1992: Refit at Hamburg.
December 1994: Further refit at Hamburg.
1999: Refit and modernization costing $90 million.
October 2008: Final transatlantic crossing.
November 2008: Final cruise: Southampton–Dubai; sold to Istithmar Corp., Dubai for $100 million; plan to be remade as museum, hotel and luxury condominiums moored on Palm Island.
2009: Plans never materialized; ship laid-up at Port Rashid, Dubai. Later plans to use the ship as a hotel in Cape Town and then in various Chinese port cities never materialized.
September 2009: Registry to Vanuatu.

2010: Plan to return ship to the U.K., moored on the Thames or at Southampton, never materialized.
September 2011: Rumored to become hotel, museum, etc. at Liverpool; never materialized.
December 2012: Reportedly sold to Chinese shipbreakers for an excessive $35 million; never materialized.
April 2016: Ship moved to inner harbor at Port Rashid, but amidst rumors to be sold to Indian scrappers.
December 2016: All davits and lifeboats fully removed.
April 2018: Partially reopened as a hotel and museum.

Different in Style and Appearance: The new *QE2*. (*Mick Lindsay collection*)

Maiden arrival at New York, May 1969. (*Mick Lindsay collection*)

Queen Mary 2 and *Queen Elizabeth 2*, April 2004. (*Cunard*)

12

Donaldson Line

Captain Cook

Service: Seven charter sailings in 1955: Glasgow–Liverpool–Quebec City–Montreal.
Particulars: 13,876 gross tons; 538 × 66 feet.
Builders: Fairfield Shipbuilding & Engineering Co., Glasgow, Scotland, 1925.
Machinery: Steam turbines; twin screw; service speed 15 knots.
Capacity: 1,088 one-class passengers.

October 14, 1924: Launched as *Letitia* for Donaldson Line, British flag.
April 25, 1925: Departed from Glasgow on maiden voyage to Canada. 516 cabin class and 1,023 tourist class.
1933: Accommodation restyled as 298 cabin class, 310 tourist class, and 964 third class.
1939–44: British Government trooping.
1944–46: Used as hospital ship.
1946: Sold to British Ministry of Transport, but managed by Donaldson Line; renamed *Empire Brent*.
1947: Refitted as peacetime troopship.
1948: U.K.–India and Far East trooping services.
1950: Glasgow–Sydney migrant service.
1951–52: Refitted at Glasgow; 1,088 one-class passengers; renamed *Captain Cook*.
1955: Chartered to Donaldson Line for seven transatlantic voyages; unsuccessful.
1956–60: Migrant service.
October 1959: Final sailing Glasgow–New Zealand; afterward charter round voyage to Malaya with New Zealand troops.
April 29, 1960: Arrived at Inverkeithing for scrapping.

Lismoria

Service: Glasgow–Montreal direct service. Until 1955, winter service to North American West Coast (Los Angeles, San Francisco, Vancouver, etc.); after 1955, to Saint John NB and Halifax.
Particulars: 8,323 gross tons; 455 × 62 × 28 feet.
Builders: California Shipbuilding Corp., Los Angeles, California, 1945.
Machinery: Steam turbines; single screw; service speed 15 knots.
Capacity: Fifty-five first-class passengers.
Notes: Former freighter rebuilt as passenger-cargo ship.

January 31, 1945: Delivered to War Shipping Administration, U.S. flag, as Victory Class freighter-transport *Taos Victory*.
1946: Transferred to British Ministry of Transport, managed by Furness Withy & Co., British flag. Refitted as a freighter.
1948: Sold to Donaldson Line, British; refitted with fifty-five passenger berths; intended to be renamed *Cabotia*, but renamed *Lismoria*.
October 10, 1948: Maiden sailing from Glasgow.
1966: Withdrawn from service; ending Donaldson passenger service.
November 1966: Sold to Astroguarda Cía Navigation S/A, Greek flag; renamed *Neon*; used as a freighter.
May 1967: Scrapped at Kaohsiung, Taiwan.

Laurentia

Service: Glasgow–Montreal (same service as *Lismoria*).
Particulars: 8,349 gross tons; 455 × 62 × 28 feet.
Builders: Permanent Shipyard No. 1, Richmond, California, 1945.
Machinery: Steam turbines; single screw; service speed 15 knots.
Capacity: Fifty-five first-class passengers.
Notes: Former freighter rebuilt as passenger-cargo ship. As built, she was the first American merchant ship fitted with radar.

March 1945: Delivered to War Shipping Administration, U.S. flag, as Victory Class freighter-transport *Medina Victory*.
June 1946: Transferred to British Ministry of Transport, managed by Donaldson Line, British flag.
September 1947: Sold to Donaldson Line; commenced refit at Barclay Curle Shipyard, Glasgow; fitted with fifty-five passenger berths; renamed *Laurentia*.
May 12, 1949: Departed Glasgow on maiden crossing to Montreal.
1966: Withdrawn from Donaldson service; later chartered to Cunard for freighter voyages to U.S. East Coast ports.
January 4, 1967: Arrived at Valencia, Spain for scrapping.

A converted Victory Ship, the *Laurentia* heads along the River Clyde in this view. (*Gillespie-Faber collection*)

13

Dutch World Services

Sibajak

Service: Occasional summer sailings between Rotterdam, Halifax, and New York; also some sailings to Quebec City.
Particulars: 12,342 gross tons; 530 × 62 feet.
Builders: De Schelde Shipyard, Flushing, Holland, 1928.
Machinery: Sulzer diesels; twin screw; service speed 17 knots.
Capacity: 1,000 one-class passengers.

April 2, 1927: Launched for Rotterdam Lloyd, Dutch flag.
February 8, 1928: Departed from Rotterdam on maiden voyage to Dutch East Indies via Suez. 527 passengers in three classes.
1935: Major refit; tonnage relisted as 12,226.
1940–48: Trooping under P&O Lines management.
1949: Refitted as migrant ship with 1,000 berths.
1950: Rotterdam–Sydney migrant sailings.
1951: Rotterdam–Indonesia service.
April 1952: Began sailings between Rotterdam and Quebec City.
May 5, 1954: Rotterdam–Halifax–New York sailings.
1955–59: Returned to Rotterdam–Indonesia service.
August 25, 1959: Arrived at Hong Kong for scrapping.

Johan van Oldenbarnevelt

Service: Occasional student and low-fare voyages between Amsterdam or Rotterdam, Southampton, and New York. Between 1959 and '62, eastbound sailings from Port Everglades and occasionally New York to Southampton and Rotterdam.
Particulars: 19,787 gross tons; 608 × 74 × 27 feet.
Builders: Netherlands Shipbuilding Co., Amsterdam, Holland, 1930.
Machinery: Sulzer diesels; twin screw; service speed 17 knots.
Capacity: 1951–59: 1,414 one-class passengers; 1959–63: 1,186 one-class passengers.

August 3, 1929: Launched; at time largest ship yet built in Holland; owned by Nederland Line, Dutch flag.
May 1930: Maiden voyage from Amsterdam to Dutch East Indies via Suez.
September 1939: Transatlantic crossing to New York for evacuation purposes on behalf of Holland–America Line.
1940: Refitted at Belfast as a troopship.
October 1945: Final trooping voyage: Bombay–Southampton.
1946: Dutch Government trooping service to/from Indonesia; also Australian migrant sailings.
1951: Refitted at Amsterdam; given 1,414 one-class berths; continued Amsterdam–Australia migrant sailings.
June 1954: One Atlantic crossing Rotterdam–Quebec City with students.
1954–58: Occasional sailings to New York; also Australian migrant sailings.
1958–59: Major refit at Amsterdam; greatly improved accommodation for 1,186 passengers; new dome-topped funnels; hull repainted in grey; tonnage relisted as 20,314.
April 1959: Commenced continuous eastabout around-the-world service in conjunction with *Oranje* and *Willem Ruys* (qv).
1963: Sold to Shipping Investment Corp (Greek Line), Greek flag; sale price $1.2 million; renamed *Lakonia;* refitted for cruise service from Southampton to the Atlantic Isles and Mediterranean.
December 22, 1963: During Christmas cruise, destroyed by fire off Madeira; 128 passengers and crew perished.
December 29, 1963: Capsized and sank 250 miles west of Gibraltar while empty and under tow.

The Dutch *Sibajak* makes periodic Atlantic crossings. (*Gillespie-Faber collection*)

New Look: Formerly the *Johan van Oldenbarnevelt*, Greek Line's *Lakonia* makes a 1962 arrival at Southampton. (*Mick Lindsay collection*)

Oranje

Service: 1959–64: Westbound voyages: Amsterdam and Southampton to Port Everglades and occasionally New York as part of westabout world voyages.
Particulars: 20,551 gross tons; 656 × 83 × 28 feet.
Builders: Netherlands Shipbuilding Co., Amsterdam, Holland, 1939.
Machinery: Sulzer diesels; triple screw; service speed 21½ knots.
Capacity: 323 first class and 626 tourist class.

September 8, 1938: Launched by HM Queen Wilhelmina; owned by Nederland Line, Dutch flag.
July 1939: Completed; world's fastest motor liner (reached 26½ knots during sea trials).
September 1939: Maiden voyage from Amsterdam to Dutch East Indies via Suez.
December 1939–February 1941: Laid-up at Surabaya for safety.
February 1941: Commenced five-month conversion to a hospital ship at Sydney.
1941–46: Hospital ship with Royal Australian Navy, but remaining under Dutch flag.
July 19, 1946: Returned to Nederland Line; refitted after war service; tonnage relisted as 20,017.
1946–50: Amsterdam–Indonesia service.
1950–58: Amsterdam–Australia and around-the-world sailings.
January 6, 1953: *Oranje* and *Willem Ruys* were to pass one another in the Red Sea off Port Sudan, but at a combined speed of 40 knots, the two liners became too close and together with interaction of the water, they collided. The two ships bumped and scraped their entire lengths, and later required lengthy repairs.
1959: Thoroughly refitted at Amsterdam; accommodation restyled for 949 passengers; tonnage relisted as 20,551.
1959–64: Continuous around-the-world sailings.
May 1962: Made special cruise from Amsterdam into North Sea with large contingent of royalty onboard for HM Queen Juliana's Silver Wedding celebration.
September 1964: Sold to Lauro Line, Italian flag; sale price $2.6 million.
1965: Renamed *Angelina Lauro*; commenced major rebuilding at Genoa; lengthened to 672 feet.

Off to Djakarta: The *Oranje* outbound at Amsterdam. (*ALF collection*)

August 24, 1965: Heavy fire damages at Genoa shipyard; six workmen killed.
March 6, 1966: Maiden voyage from Bremerhaven to Australia via Suez; 189 first class and 1,427 tourist class passengers; tonnage relisted as 24,377.
1973: Cruising only: 800 one-class passengers.
October 1977: Commenced three-year charter to Costa Line; marketed as *Angelina*; winter Caribbean cruises from San Juan, summer Mediterranean cruises from Genoa.
March 31, 1979: Gutted by fire at St. Thomas berth; total loss.
May 26, 1979: Salvage commenced.
July 2, 1979: First raised.
July 6, 1979: Fully refloated.
July 30, 1979: Left St. Thomas under tow of Japanese tug *Nippon Maru*; bound for scrapping at Kaohsiung.
September 24, 1979: Sank while empty and under tow in mid Pacific.

Willem Ruys

Service: 1959–64: Port Everglades, Bermuda and occasionally New York to Southampton and Rotterdam as part of continuous eastabout around-the-world voyages.
Particulars: 23,114 gross tons; 631 × 82 × 29 feet.
Builders: De Schelde Shipyard, Flushing, Holland, 1947.
Machinery: Sulzer diesels; twin screw; service speed 22 knots.
Capacity: 275 first class and 770 tourist class.
May 7, 1938: Ordered.
January 25, 1939: Laid down; for Rotterdam Lloyd, Dutch flag; intended to be named *Ardjoeno*.
1940–45: Construction slowed owing to Nazi occupation of Holland.
1946: Construction resumed; name changed to *Willem Ruys*.
July 1, 1946: Launched.
November 1947: Trials; attained top speed of 24.6 knots.
November 21, 1947: Rotterdam Lloyd renamed Royal Rotterdam Lloyd prior to ship's maiden voyage.
December 1947: Maiden voyage: Rotterdam-Indonesia.
January 6, 1953: *Willem Ruys* collided with *Oranje* in Red Sea; serious damages.
June 1958: First sailing to New York; plus two charter sailings for Europe–Canada Line from Rotterdam to Montreal.
September 20, 1958–February 25, 1959: Major refit at Schiedam; passenger accommodation modernized; funnels raised in height; tonnage relisted from 21,119 to 23,114.
March 1959: Began new around-the-world service.
December 1964: Sold to Lauro Line, Italian flag; sale price $6.8 million.
1965: Commenced extensive refit at Palermo; renamed *Achille Lauro*.
August 29, 1965: Badly damaged by fire at shipyard at Palermo. Later repaired; extensively refitted and modernized including new fin-topped funnels; tonnage increased to 23,629; 152 first class and approximately 1,500 tourist class passengers.

April 7, 1966: Began first voyage between North Europe and Australia via Suez.
May 19, 1972: Heavy damage by fire at Genoa; later repaired.
December 1972: Cruise service only hereafter.
April 28, 1975: Collided with and sank small Lebanese freighter *Youssef* off Turkish coast.
January 23, 1982: Lauro Line in financial difficulties; ship detained for debt at Tenerife during Cape Town–Genoa voyage.
January 28, 1983: Arrived at Genoa; laid-up.
1984: Resumed sailing; Mediterranean cruises from Genoa.
October 8, 1985: Ship seized by Arab terrorists; one passenger killed. Terrorists surrendered on October 9; ship returned to Genoa on October 16.
1987: Transferred to StarLauro Cruises (Mediterranean Shipping Co.), Italian flag.
November 30, 1994: Caught fire from an engine explosion while off Somalia during a Genoa–Durban voyage; later abandoned.
December 2, 1994: Empty and drifting; later sank.

Dutch Style: The *Willem Ruys* at Southampton. (*Mick Lindsay collection*)

The same ship but as the greatly rebuilt *Achille Lauro*. (*Mick Lindsay collection*)

14

East Asiatic Co.

Erria

Service: Copenhagen–New York/U.S. East Coast ports (variously via Copenhagen, Aarhus, Gothenburg, Oslo, Middlesbrough, Antwerp, Bremen, Hamburg, Rotterdam, and Dover—and in the U.S. to Boston, Philadelphia, Baltimore, Norfolk, and Charleston)
Particulars: 7,670 gross tons; 463 × 62 × 25 feet.
Builders: Nakskov Skibsværft, Nakskov, Denmark, 1932.
Machinery: B&W type diesels; twin screw; service speed 16 knots.
Capacity: Seventy-four first class passengers.
Notes: "Funnel-less" ship; exhausts worked through mast.

1934–39: Copenhagen–Far East via Suez service.
1940–45: Laid-up during war years.
1946–49: Copenhagen–Far East service.
1949–51: Occasional Copenhagen–New York sailings.
October 21, 1950: Rammed by freighter *Pelican State* near New York harbor; damaged; later repaired.
December 1951: Badly damaged by fire while at sea off Portland, Oregon; salvaged and later repaired at Schiedam, Holland but rebuilt as a freighter without passenger quarters.
1952–62: Copenhagen–Far East service.
1962: Scrapped at Osaka, Japan.

Jutlandia

Service: Copenhagen–New York and other U.S. East Coast ports (same as for *Erria*).
Particulars: 8,542 gross tons; 460 × 61 × 25 feet.
Builders: Nakskov Skibsværft, Nakskov, Denmark, 1934.
Machinery: B&W type diesels; twin screw; service speed 14 knots.
Capacity: Sixty-nine all-first class passengers.
Notes: "Funnel-less" ship; exhausts worked through mast.
1934–39: Copenhagen–Far East via Suez service.
1940–45: Laid-up during the war.
March 1946: Began Copenhagen–New York sailings.
1950: Withdrawn from transatlantic service; converted to hospital ship for use during Korean War.
1954–64: Refitted and resumed Copenhagen–Far East service; occasionally used as Danish royal yacht.
January 9, 1965: Arrived at Bilbao, Spain for scrapping.

Falstria

Service: Copenhagen–New York and/or other U.S. East Coast ports (same itinerary as *Erria*).

Particulars: 6,993 gross tons; 453 × 63 × 25 feet.
Builders: Nakskov Skibsværft, Nakskov, Denmark, 1941–45.
Machinery: B&W type diesels; single screw; service speed 15 knots.
Capacity: Fifty-four first class passengers.
Notes: "Funnel-less" ship; exhausts worked through mast.

1941: Launched; then laid-up owing to the war.
May 1945: Damaged during Allied air attacks on Nakskov.
November 1945: Completed; entered Copenhagen–Far East service.
1952: Some Copenhagen–New York sailings.
1953: Resumed Copenhagen–Far East service.
1964: Sold to Greek buyers; renamed *Veryr*; resold to Japanese shipbreakers.

The four-masted *Jutlandia* berthed at Vancouver. (*Gillespie-Faber collection*)

15

Europe-Canada Line

Seven Seas

Service: Bremerhaven and/or Rotterdam, Le Havre, and Southampton to Quebec City and Montreal or Halifax (westbound only) and New York. Winter: Around-the-world cruises as "floating university."
Particulars: 12,575 gross tons; 492 × 69 × 22 feet.
Builders: Sun Shipbuilding & Dry Dock Co., Chester, Pennsylvania, 1940.
Machinery: Sulzer diesels; single screw; service speed 16½ knots.
Capacity: Twenty first class and 987 tourist class.
Notes: Former freighter and aircraft carrier rebuilt as a passenger ship.

1940: Completed as *Mormacmail*, C3-class freighter for Moore-McCormack Lines, U.S. flag.
March 6, 1941: Transferred to U.S. Navy and rebuilt in seventy-seven days as first auxiliary aircraft carrier.
June 2, 1941: Commissioned as *USS Long Island*.
1941–46: Military service.
April 1946: Decommissioned; laid-up.
April 1947: Declared surplus; sold to shipbreakers at Portland, Oregon; demolition delayed.
March 1948: Sold to Caribbean Land & Shipping Co., Panamanian flag; renamed *Nelly*; rebuilt as migrant carrier with 1,300 berths by Albina Engineering & Machine Works at Portland.
1949–53: Migrant sailings to Australia, New York, and Canada.
1953: Sold to Europe-Canada Line (joint creation of Holland-America Line and Royal Rotterdam Lloyd), Panamanian flag; renamed *Seven Seas*; refitted with upgraded accommodation.
April 30, 1955: Maiden sailing from Bremerhaven to Montreal.
July 1955: Transferred to West German flag; to be renamed *Bremen*, but did not materialize.
July 18, 1965: Immobilized by engine room fire while in North Atlantic; repairs lasted until June 1966.
September 1966: Became moored hostel at Rotterdam for foreign workers of Verolme Shipyards.
May 4, 1977: Left Rotterdam under tow for Ghent to be scrapped.

The converted *Seven Seas* outbound at Southampton. (*Mick Lindsay collection*)

16

French Line

De Grasse

Service: Le Havre, Southampton, or Plymouth, New York.
Particulars: 18,435 gross tons; 574 × 71 × 29 feet.
Builders: Cammell Laird & Co. Ltd., Birkenhead, England, 1924.
Machinery: Steam turbines; twin screw; service speed 16 knots.
Capacity: 500 first class and 470 tourist class.

1918: Laid down as *Suffren,* French Line, French flag; construction delayed owing to World War I.
February 23, 1924: Launched as *De Grasse.*
August 21, 1924: Left Le Havre on maiden voyage to New York; 17,707 gross tons; 536 cabin class and 410 third class passengers.
1936: Proposed California–South Pacific–Australia service; never materialized.
1940: Seized by Nazi invasion forces and used as accommodation ship in the River Gironde near Bordeaux.
August 30, 1944: Scuttled at Bordeaux by retreating Nazi forces.
August 30, 1945: Salvaged; later towed to Saint-Nazaire; repaired and restored with one funnel. Tonnage relisted as 18,435; 970 passengers in two classes.
July 12, 1947: Departed Le Havre on first post-war voyage to New York.
September 30, 1951: Last sailing from New York to Le Havre.
April 1952: Assigned to fulltime Le Havre–West Indies service.
March 26, 1953: Sold to Canadian Pacific Steamships Ltd., British flag; renamed *Empress of Australia* (qv).

Île de France

Service: Le Havre, Southampton, or Le Havre, New York. Winter cruising.
Particulars: 44,356 gross tons; 792 × 91 × 30 feet.
Builders: Chantiers de l'Atlantique, Saint-Nazaire, France, 1927.
Machinery: Steam turbines; quadruple screw; service speed 23½ knots.
Capacity: 541 first class, 577 cabin class, and 227 tourist class.
Notes: One of the most illustrious and popular liners ever built.

March 14, 1926: Launched; built for French Line, French flag.
June 22, 1927: Departed Le Havre on maiden voyage to New York; 43,153 gross tons; 670 first class, 408 second class and 508 third class.
November 1932–April 1933: Major refit in attempt to reduce great vibration.
September 1939: Laid-up at New York for safety.
May 1940: Began troopship service.
July 19, 1940: Seized at Singapore by British forces; managed hereafter by Cunard-White Star.
September 22, 1945: Reverted to French flag, but under Cunard management.
October 22, 1946: Began austerity service between Cherbourg and New York.
April 1947: Commenced refit at Saint-Nazaire; three funnels reduced to two; tonnage relisted as 44,356; passenger accommodation modernized.
July 21, 1949: Left Le Havre on first post-war luxury crossing.
July 26, 1956: Rescued 753 survivors from *Andrea Doria-Stockholm* collision off Nantucket.
February 1957: Went aground on Martinique during Caribbean cruise; damaged; towed to Newport News Shipyard in Virginia for repairs.
November 10, 1958: Departed New York on final crossing to Le Havre.
December 1958: Laid-up at Le Havre and offered for sale; later sold to Japanese shipbreakers.
February 26, 1959: Departed Le Havre for Osaka as *Furansu Maru*, Japanese flag, for scrapping.
April 9, 1959: Arrived at Osaka; later used as floating set in film *The Last Voyage*.
September 1959: Demolition completed.

Top left: Heading for a winter's cruise to the Caribbean, the *Île de France* passes along an ice-filled Hudson River. (*ALF collection*)

Above: The *Liberté*'s maiden arrival at New York in August 1950. (*ALF collection*)

Left: Partially sunk, the bow section of the *Liberté* with the sunken remains of the liner *Paris* on the left. (*Author's collection*)

Liberté

Service: Le Havre, Southampton, or Plymouth, New York.
Particulars: 51,839 gross tons; 936 × 102 × 34 feet.
Builders: Blohm & Voss A/G, Hamburg, Germany, 1930.
Machinery: Steam turbines; quadruple screw; service speed 24 knots.
Capacity: 555 first class, 497 cabin class, and 450 tourist class.
Notes: Briefly captured Blue Riband in 1930 and became world's fastest liner; French flagship and largest liner 1946–61.

August 15, 1928: Launched as *Europa* for North German Lloyd, German flag.
March 26, 1929: Nearly destroyed by fire at shipyard; subsequently repaired. 49,746 gross tons; 2,024 passengers in four classes.
March 19, 1930: Left Bremerhaven on maiden voyage to New York; captured Blue Riband with average speed of 27.9 knots.
September 1939: Laid-up at Bremerhaven; later fitted out for intention Nazi invasion of Britain.
1940: Considered for conversion to aircraft carrier; never materialized.
May 1945: Seized by invading American forces at Bremerhaven; became troopship *USS Europa*, Transatlantic troop service but plagued with small fires. Carried some eastbound passengers for United States Lines. Later considered for restoration under U.S. flag; never materialized.
June 1946: Awarded by United Nations Reparations Committee to France; transferred to French Line; intended name *Lorraine*, then *Liberation* and *La Liberation*, *La Liberté* but *Liberté* finally selected.
December 9, 1946: Broke away from moorings at Le Havre during storm; slammed against the sunken wreckage of the liner *Paris*; *Liberté* partially sunk.

The *Flandre* and her sister ship *Antilles* "nested" together at Le Havre. (*Author's collection*)

In 1969, the ex-*Flandre* was sailed as the *Princess Carla* for Los Angeles-based Princess Cruises. She is seen here off San Pedro. (*Princess Cruises*)

April 15, 1947: Fully refloated; towed to Saint-Nazaire for thorough refitting; cost $19 million.
August 17, 1950: Left Le Havre on maiden crossing to New York; tonnage relisted as 51,839.
February 1954: Funnels raised in height with dome tops.
November 1961: Final sailing from New York to Le Havre; rumored to become a floating hotel at Seattle for 1962 World's Fair.
December 1962: Sold to West India Shipping & Trading Co., Vaduz, Liechtenstein.
January 30, 1962: Arrived at La Spezia, Italy for scrapping.
June 1962: Demolition completed.

Flandre

Service: Le Havre, Southampton, or Plymouth, New York. Winter: Le Havre–West Indies or cruising.
Particulars: 20,477 gross tons; 600 × 80 × 26 feet.
Builders: Ateliers et Chantiers de France, Dunkirk, France, 1952.
Machinery: Steam turbines; twin screw; twin screw.
Capacity: 402 first class, 389 cabin class, and 97 tourist class as built; after 1953: 339 first class, 285 tourist class, and 100 interchangeable.

October 31, 1951: Launched.
July 23, 1952: Departed Le Havre on maiden voyage to New York; engine room breakdown off New York, towed into port. Returned to builders for major overhaul.
April 17, 1953: Commenced second maiden voyage from Le Havre to New York.
1955: Accommodation restyled as 232 first class and 511 tourist class.
October 1962: Reassigned to fulltime Le Havre–West Indies; repainted with white hull.
1967: Summer crossings to Montreal for Expo 67.
February 1968: Sold to Costa Line, Italian flag; renamed

Carla C. Refitted for year-round cruising; 19,975 gross tons; 754 one-class passengers.
February 1968: Entered cruise service.
January 1969: Began charter to Princess Cruises; advertised as *Princess Carla*; Los Angeles–Mexico and Caribbean sailings.
1970: Returned to Costa for Caribbean cruises from San Juan.
June 1, 1974: Arrived at Amsterdam for conversion to motor liner.
January 1975: Resumed cruising with new Stork-Werkspoor diesels.
1983: Tonnage relisted as 19,942.
1986: Renamed *Carla Costa.*
1992: Sold to Epirotiki Lines, Greek flag; renamed *Pallas Athena*; used for seven-day cruises to the Eastern Mediterranean from Piraeus.
March 28, 1994: Totally destroyed by fire at Piraeus; declared a complete loss.
December 25, 1994: Arrived under tow at Aliağa, Turkey, to be scrapped.

France

Service: Le Havre, Southampton, New York; winter cruising.
Particulars: 66,348 gross tons; 1,035 × 110 × 34 feet.
Builders: Chantiers de l'Atlantique, Saint-Nazaire, France, 1962.
Machinery: Steam turbines; quadruple screw; service speed 30 knots.
Capacity: 501 first class and 1,443 tourist class; 1,349 one-class during cruises.

July 26, 1956: Ordered.
October 7, 1957: Keel laid.
May 11, 1960: Launched and named by Madame Yvonne de Gaulle.
November 1961: Trial cruise from Le Havre.
February 3, 1962: Left Le Havre on maiden voyage to New York.
November 9, 1968: Completed millionth mile sea mile; carried 412,097 passengers since 1962. Highly successful.
November 20, 1969: First sailing from Bremerhaven; thereafter, transatlantic crossings occasionally extended.
January 1972: Left New York on first world cruise.
September 1974: Seized by union seamen and anchored in the English Channel near Le Havre; surrendered to French Line officials on October 9.
October 1974: Withdrawn from service and laid-up at Le Havre.

The stunning *France* well underway. (*ALF collection*)

1975: Sold to Saudi Arabian businessman Akram Ojjeh for $22 million. Proposed use as hotel-casino-museum of French culture failed to materialize; ship continued in lay-up at Le Havre.
June 1979: Sold to Norwegian Caribbean Lines, Norwegian flag; renamed *Norway*; sale price $18 million.
August 18, 1979: Left Le Havre under tow for Bremerhaven.
August 22, 1979: Commenced major refits at Hapag-Lloyd shipyard at Bremerhaven; costing in excess of $150 million; restyled as year-round cruise ship. Only one engine room and thereby conserving fuel; service speed 16–18 knots (maximum speed 25 knots).
April 14, 1980 Apr: First trails after refit; tonnage relisted as 70,202.
April 24, 1980: Transferred to Norwegian owners; completion of refit. Gross tonnage increased to 69,500, becoming world's largest passenger liner; passenger capacity to 2,181 one-class; crew reduced to 800.
May 1980: Transatlantic crossing: Oslo–Southampton–New York.

June 1980: First weekly cruise from Miami.
April–July 1982: Major refit at Bremerhaven; partial diesels installed.
September 1984: First diesel installation at Hamburg.
1990: Transferred to Bahamian registry.
September 1990: Major refit at Bremerhaven and two new decks added; capacity increased to 2,565; tonnage relisted as 76,049.
September 2001: Transatlantic cruise.
May 26, 2003: Serious explosion at Miami.
June 2003: Sailed empty from Miami to Bremerhaven; laid-up.
May 2005: Towed from Bremerhaven to Port Klang with intention to be restored for Star Cruises and short gambling cruises; plans later dropped.
February 2006: Renamed *Blue Lady.* Further plans to use her as moored hotel and casino in Malaysia failed to materialize.
August 15, 2006: Beached at Alang in preparation for scrapping.

Above: The French flagship arrives at Southampton. (*Mick Lindsay collection*)

Right: The newly refitted *Liberté*, outbound in August 1950, passes the inbound *Île de France*. (*Moran Towing & Transportation Co.*)

Vastly changed, the former *France* as the *Norway* arrives at New York for a second maiden welcome in May 1980. (*Author's collection*)

17

Furness-Warren Line

Nova Scotia

Service: Liverpool to St. John NF, Halifax, and Boston.
Particulars: 7,438 gross tons; 440 × 61 × 25 feet.
Builders: Vickers-Armstrong Shipbuilders Ltd., Newcastle, England, 1947.
Machinery: Steam turbines; single screw; service speed 15 knots.
Capacity: Sixty-two first class and ninety-two tourist class.
Notes: Ice-strengthened hull.

September 2, 1947: Left Liverpool on maiden voyage to Canada and Boston.
1961: Reduced to twelve-passenger freighter.
1962: Sold to Dominion Far East Line, Bahamas flag; renamed *Francis Drake*. 130 first class passengers; Australia–Far East–Japan service.
March 18, 1971: Arrived at Kaohsiung, Taiwan, for scrapping.

Newfoundland

Service: Liverpool to St. John NF, Halifax, and Boston.
Particulars: 7,437 gross tons; 440 × 61 × 25 feet.
Builders: Vickers-Armstrong Shipbuilders Ltd., Newcastle, England, 1948.
Machinery: Steam turbines; single screw; service speed 15 knots.
Capacity: Sixty-two first class and ninety-two tourist class.
Notes: Ice-strengthened hull.

February 14, 1947: Left Liverpool on maiden voyage to Canada and Boston.
1961: Reduced to twelve-passenger freighter.
1962: Sold to Dominion Far East Line, Bahamas flag; renamed *George Anson*. 130 first class passengers; Australia–Far East–Japan service.
February 15, 1971: Arrived at Kaohsiung, Taiwan, for scrapping.

The *Newfoundland* berthed at Liverpool. (*Kenneth Wrightman collection, courtesy of Mick Lindsay*)

18

German Atlantic Line

Hanseatic (1964)

Service: Cuxhaven (Hamburg), Southampton, New York; winter cruising.
Particulars: 25,338 gross tons; 629 × 82 × 26 feet.
Builders: Chantiers de l'Atlantique, Saint-Nazaire, France, 1964.
Machinery: Steam turbines; twin screw; service speed 20 knots.
Capacity: 148 first class and 864 tourist class; 650 one-class for cruises.

1964–67: Sailed as *Shalom*, Zim Lines, Israeli flag (qv).
May 1967: Acquired from Zim Lines.
November 1967: Formally transferred to German-Atlantic Line, West German flag; renamed *Hanseatic*.
December 1967: Maiden cruise.
1969–73: Cruising only.
August 1973: Sold to Home Lines.
September 25, 1973: Transferred to Home Lines at Genoa; Panamanian flag; refitted for 945 one-class passengers; renamed *Doric*.
January 1974: Entered winter service from Port Everglades to the Caribbean; summers (April–November) New York–Bermuda cruises.
January 1981: Sold to Lido Maritime Inc., Greek flag; later renamed *Royal Odyssey* for operation by Royal Cruise Lines.
January–May 1982: Extensive refit including new funnel; 817 all-one class passengers.
July 10, 1984: Collided with and sank Soviet freighter *Vasya Alekseyev*; *Royal Odyssey* later repaired at Hamburg.
December 1988: Sold to Regency Cruises, Bahamian flag; renamed *Regent Sun*.
1995: Collapse of Regency Cruises; ship laid-up.
1997: Auctioned-off to International Shipping Partners, Bahamian flag; renamed *Sun*.
2000: Plan to restore ship as floating spa; to be renamed *Canyon Ranch at Sea*; never materialized.
July 26, 2001: Sank off South Africa while empty and under tow; bound for Alang, India, to be scrapped.

German-Atlantic Line's *Hanseatic* but seen as Royal Cruise Lines' *Royal Odyssey*. (*Royal Cruise Lines*)

Hamburg

Service: Occasional positioning voyages: Cuxhaven, Southampton, New York; mostly cruising.
Particulars: 24,962 gross tons; 642 × 90 feet.
Builders: Deutsche Werft Shipyard, Hamburg, Germany, 1969.
Machinery: Steam turbines; twin screw; service speed 21 knots.
Capacity: 600 one-class passengers (790 maximum berths).
Notes: West Germany's first newly built luxury liner.

April 1, 1966: Ordered.
February 21, 1968: Launched; intended service Cuxhaven–Southampton–New York with only winter cruising; near completion, operations revised to fulltime cruising.
January 1969: Delayed by turbine problems.
March 1969: Delivered.

The innovative *Hamburg* arriving at Los Angeles. (*German-Atlantic Line*)

Dominated by her unique funnel, the former *Hamburg* is seen in her later years as the *Maxim Gorky*. (*Mick Lindsay collection*)

March 30, 1969: Left Cuxhaven on maiden cruise to South America.
June 1969: Maiden sailing to New York.
February 7, 1972: Began seasonal cruising from San Francisco and Los Angeles.
September 1973: Renamed *Hanseatic* for further cruising.
December 1973: Withdrawn from service; laid-up. Later reportedly sold to Ryutsu Kaiun KK, Japanese flag for approximately $30 million; never materialized. Later sold to Robin International, Liberian flag as agents for Black Sea Steamship Co., Soviet flag; renamed *Maxim Gorky*.
February 19, 1974: Left Southampton under charter to United Artists Films for use as floating prop in film *Juggernaut*; temporarily renamed *Britannic*.
1974–75: Cruising from New York.
November 1975: Damaged by bomb explosion at San Juan.
December 1975: Transferred to European charter cruising mostly for West German companies (including Neckermann and Phoenix Reisen).
1988–89: Major refit and modernization at Bremerhaven.
June 19, 1989: Nearly sank after colliding with drifting ice in Spitzbergen; ship evacuated and later patched and then towed to Bremerhaven for full repairs.
July 26, 1991: Fire in crew quarters.
1991: Changed to Cypriot owners, Bahamian flag; chartered for cruising.
November 2008: Final charter cruise for Phoenix Reisen.
December 2008: Laid-up at Eleusis, Greece pending sale. Rumored to become museum ship at Hamburg; also later to be refitted as the *Marco Polo* for revived Orient Line; neither materialized.
January 2009: Sold to Liberian intermediary buyers for Indian scrappers.
February 24, 2009: Arrived at Alang as renamed *Maxim M* to be beached and then scrapped.

19

Greek Line

Canberra (1913)

Service: Seasonally between Bremerhaven, Southampton, Cherbourg, Cobh, and Montreal; laid-up during winter.
Particulars: 7,707 gross tons; 426 × 57 feet.
Builders: Alexander Stephen & Sons Ltd., Glasgow, Scotland, 1913.
Machinery: Quadruple expansion engines; twin screw; service speed 15 knots.
Capacity: Sixty-four first class and 646 tourist class.

1913: Completed as *Canberra* for Australian Steamships Proprietary Ltd., Australian flag; used on Queensland coastal trade.
1917–19: Used as a troopship.
1919–39: Australian coastal service.
1939–45: Troopship.
1945: Laid-up.
1947: Reportedly sold to Chinese buyers; sailed to Singapore; sale failed to materialize. Later sold to Greek Line (Goulandris Group), Panamanian flag; retained original name; Mediterranean–Australia or Central America migrant sailings.
1949: Refitted as an oil burner (formerly coal); transferred to Piraeus–Genoa–New York service.
1951: Commenced Bremerhaven–Montreal sailings.
October 1954: Final Greek Line crossing: Quebec City–Bremerhaven.
December 1954: Sod to Dominican Republic buyers, Dominican flag; renamed *España*; Spain–West Indies migrant service.
1959: Scrapped in Dominican Republic.

Columbia

Service: Mostly seasonal: Bremerhaven, Southampton, Cherbourg, Cobh, Montreal; laid-up in winter.
Particulars: 9,424 gross tons; 466 × 60 feet.
Builders: Harland & Wolff Ltd., Belfast, Northern Ireland, 1913.
Machinery: Combination triple expansion and steam turbine engines; triple screw; service speed 15 knots.
Capacity: Fifty-two first class and 754 tourist class.

1913: Completed as *Katoomba* for McIlwraith McEacharn Proprietary Ltd., Australian flag; Sydney–Fremantle service.
1915–18: Troopship.

Dating from 1913, Greek Line's *Canberra* was one of the smallest passenger ships serving on the North Atlantic. (*Alex Duncan*)

Another veteran ship, the *Columbia* is seen at Cherbourg. (*Gillespie-Faber collection*)

1918–40: Australian coastal service.
1940–46: Troopship.
October 1946: Sold to Compañía Marítima del Este (Greek Line), Panamanian flag; sailed Sydney–Suez–Piraeus.
December 31, 1946: Piraeus–Genoa–Oran–New York sailings.
1947–49: Chartered to French Line for Le Havre–West Indies sailings.
1949: Refitted at Genoa; accommodation improved; renamed *Columbia*. Began Genoa–Australia sailings.
June 10, 1950: Commenced Greek Line service: Bremerhaven–Montreal.
December 31, 1952: Damaged by fire at Bremerhaven.
1954: Transferred to Neptunia Shipping Co. (also Greek Line), Panamanian flag.
1957: Mostly Liverpool–Quebec City sailings.
July 18, 1957: Fire at Quebec City.
August 1957: Grazed by *Homeric* in fog.
December 1957: Laid-up at Piraeus.
August 22, 1959: Left Piraeus for Nagasaki, Japan for scrapping.
September 29, 1959: Arrived at Nagasaki.

Neptunia

Service: 1949–51: Piraeus–Genoa–New York; 1951–55: Bremerhaven–Southampton–Cherbourg–New York; 1955–57: Bremerhaven–Southampton–Quebec City–Montreal. Occasional winter cruising.
Particulars: 10,519 gross tons; 523 × 59 feet.
Builders: Netherlands Shipbuilding Co., Amsterdam, Holland, 1920.
Machinery: Steam triple-expansion engines; twin screw; service speed 15 knots.
Capacity: Thirty-nine first class and 748 tourist class.

May 2, 1919: Launched as *Johan de Witt*, Nederland Line, Dutch flag.
July 1920: Entered Amsterdam–East Indies service; 197 first class, 120 second class and thirty-six third class.
December 1930–November 1932: Laid-up owing to the Depression.
November 1932: Resumed East Indies sailings.
April–October 1933: Major refit at Amsterdam; lengthened from 499 to 523 feet.
May 1940: Laid-up for safety in the Dutch East Indies; later refitted as a troopship at Sydney for British Ministry of War Transport; managed by the Orient Line.
1945: Decommissioned; laid-up.
December 15, 1948: Sold to Compañía Marítima Del Este (Greek Line), Panamanian flag; renamed *Neptunia*. Major refit: second funnel removed as well as mainmast; accommodation enlarged for thirty-nine first class and 748 tourist class.
1949: Piraeus–New York sailings.
April 8, 1951: Left New York on first voyage to Bremerhaven.
1954: Transferred to Neptunia Shipping Co. (Greek Line), retaining Panama registry.
April 1955: Commenced Bremerhaven–Montreal service.
November 2, 1957: Struck Daunts Rock, near Cobh; beached; total loss.
March 2, 1958: Towed to Rotterdam for scrapping.

Nea Hellas/New York

Service: 1947–54: Piraeus–Malta–Naples–Lisbon–Halifax (westbound only)–New York; 1955–59: New York–Boston (occasionally)–Cobh–Cherbourg–Southampton–Bremerhaven (westbound include Halifax instead of Boston).
Particulars: 16,991 gross tons; 578 × 70 × 29 feet.
Builders: Fairfield Shipbuilding & Engineering Co., Glasgow, Scotland, 1922.
Machinery: Steam turbines; twin screw; service speed 16 knots.
Capacity: 1939–54: 179 first class, 404 cabin class, and 1,399 tourist class; 1955–59:
Seventy first class and 1,300 tourist class.

October 4, 1921: Launched as *Tuscania*, Anchor Line, British flag.
September 16, 1922: Maiden voyage from Glasgow to New York; 240 first class, 377 second class and 1,818 third class.
1926–30: Chartered to Cunard Line for London–New York service.

Right: The *New York* visiting Boston. (*ALF collection*)

Below: Busy Day on a July Afternoon in 1956: The *New York* is on the right, the *Flandre* and *Queen Elizabeth* behind, and farther behind is the *Ryndam* and *Giulio Cesare*. (*Port Authority of New York & New Jersey*)

October 1930–August 1931: Laid-up owing to Depression.
1931–39: Diverse operations: Atlantic crossings, cruises, Liverpool–Suez–Bombay service.
1939: Sold to General Steam Navigation Co. of Greece (Greek Line), Greek flag; renamed *Nea Hellas*.
May 1939: Commenced Piraeus–New York sailings.
1941–47: Trooping for British Ministry of War Transport.
1947: Refitted.
August 1947: Resumed Piraeus–New York sailings.
1954–55: Major refit; renamed *New York*.
March 1955: Commenced Bremerhaven–New York service.
October 1959: Final Greek Line sailing: Quebec City–Piraeus.
November 14, 1959: Laid-up at Piraeus.
October 12, 1961: Arrived at Onomichi, Japan, for scrapping.

Arkadia

Service: Bremerhaven–Amsterdam–London–Le Havre–Cobh–Quebec City–Montreal; occasional sailings from Boston. Cruising from Boston as well as from Southampton to Atlantic Isles, West Africa, etc.
Particulars: 20,259 gross tons; 590 × 84 × 26 feet.
Builders: Vickers-Armstrong Shipbuilders Ltd., Newcastle, England, 1931.
Machinery: Steam turbo-electric engines; quadruple screw; service speed 19 knots.
Capacity: 150 first class and 1,150 tourist class; after 1961: Fifty first class and 1,337 tourist class.

The rebuilt *Arkadia* pauses at Le Havre. (*Gillespie-Faber collection*)

March 17, 1931: Launched as *Monarch of Bermuda* (original intention was to name her *Mid-Ocean*) for Furness-Bermuda Line, British flag.
December 1931: Commenced New York–Bermuda service; 22,434 gross tons; 830 passengers.
November 1939: Became troopship.
March 24, 1947: Gutted by fire during post-war refit at Newcastle; hulk laid-up in Firth of Forth. Might have been scrapped, but sold to British Ministry of Transport; towed to Southampton. Completely rebuilt as migrant ship *New Australia*; one funnel plus unique dipod mast-funnel replaced original three funnels; 20,256 gross tons; 1,600 one-class passengers.
August 1950: Commenced Southampton–Sydney sailings (also later some trooping for British Government), managed by Shaw Savill Line. Original intention was for three annual Australian round voyages and summers on the North Atlantic, but changed to four annual Australian voyages.
January 1958: Sold to Greek Line, Greek flag; renamed *Arkadia*. Major refit at Hamburg: Accommodation much improved; new bow increasing length from 579 to 590 feet. Later entered Canadian service.
February 1959: Some Caribbean cruising from New York.
1961: Refit at Hamburg; further improvements to accommodation.
May–July 1965: Mechanical troubles; withdrawn from service for repairs.
November 21, 1966: Withdrawn: laid-up in River Fal.
December 18, 1966: Arrived at Valencia, Spain, for scrapping.

Skaubryn

Service: Chartered to Greek Line in 1957: Bremerhaven–Le Havre–Southampton–Quebec City–Montreal sailings.
Particulars: 9,786 gross tons; 458 × 57 feet.
Builders: Götaverken Shipyard, Gothenburg, Sweden, 1951.
Machinery: Diesels; twin screw; service speed 16½ knots.
Capacity: 1,205 one-class passengers.
Notes: Former cargo ship.

March 1951: Completed as a freighter for I. M. Skaugen & Co., Norwegian flag; quickly rebuilt as migrant ship by Howaldtswerke Shipyard A/G, Kiel, West Germany.
1951–57: Europe–Australia and charter migrant and low-fare sailings.
June 18, 1957: Commenced Greek Line charter for Bremerhaven–Montreal service.
March 31, 1958: Caught fire in Indian Ocean during Bremerhaven–Australia sailing; abandoned but then taken in tow.
April 6, 1958: Sank while under tow.

Olympia

Service: 1953–54: Bremerhaven-Southampton–Le Havre–Cobh–Halifax (westbound only)–New York; 1955–70: New York–occasionally Boston–Azores–Lisbon–Naples–Messina–Piraeus–occasionally Limassol and Haifa; westbound Halifax instead of Boston. Winter cruising to the Caribbean and Mediterranean.
Particulars: 22,979 gross tons; 611 × 79 × 28 feet.
Builders: Alexander Stephen & Sons Ltd., Glasgow, Scotland, 1953.
Machinery: Steam turbines; twin screw; service speed 22 knots.
Capacity: 138 first class and 1,169 tourist class.
Notes: First new liner built for Greek owners.

April 16, 1953: Launched as Number 636. Intended name *Frederica*; dispute ensued with Greek Government over

Right: The Norwegian-owned *Skaubryn* was chartered to the Greek Line. (*Halifax Maritime Museum*)

Below: Burning in the Indian Ocean. (*ALF collection*)

Greek registry; ship named *Olympia* instead; Liberian registry. Hull rumored to have been that of incomplete Royal Navy aircraft carrier.
October 15, 1953: Departed from Glasgow on extended maiden voyage to New York via Belfast, Liverpool, Southampton, Cherbourg, Cobh, and Halifax.
October 1953: Aground at Southampton.
March 1, 1954: Turbine trouble in the Caribbean during cruise.
March 1955: Transferred to New York–Piraeus service.
June 1961: Turbine trouble off Halifax.
November–December 1961: Major refit at Genoa.
September 27, 1968: Transferred to Greek flag while at Pier 97, New York.
1970: Major refit; mainmast removed; accommodation modernized; 1,037 one-class passengers for fulltime cruising.
March 24, 1974: Laid-up in Perama Bay, Greece; collapse of Greek Line in Jan 1975; ship seized by Greek authorities and banks; offered fosale.
June 1980: Reported to have been sold to Sheraton Hotel Corp for use in seven-day Caribbean cruise service as *Sheraton Caribbean;* never materialized.
1981: Sold to Sally Shipping Co., West German flag; renamed *Caribe*; but remained laid-up at Piraeus.
March 11, 1983: Arrived at Hamburg under tow; rebuilt; new funnel; refitted with diesel machinery; accommodation restyled for 1,200 passengers.
June 29, 1983: Completed as *Caribe I*; later sailed to Miami for weekly Caribbean cruise service.
1983: Owners relisted as Hanseatic Caribbean Shipping Co. Inc., Panamanian flag.
1985: Owners relisted as Olympia Shipping Co. Inc., Panamanian flag.
May 1988: Conventional funnel added during refit at Norfolk.
1993: Sold to Regal Cruise Lines, Bahamian flag; renamed *Regal Empress*.
1995: Tonnage listed as 21,909.
April 2003: Sold to Imperial Majesty Cruise Lines, Bahamian flag; used for short cruises between Port Everglades and Nassau.
September–October 2008: Used as accommodation ship at Galveston.
December 2008: Resumed short cruising from Port Everglades.
March 2009: Withdrawn from service.
July 23, 2009: Arrived at Alang to be scrapped.

Queen Anna Maria

Service: New York–occasionally Boston–Azores–Lisbon–Naples–Messina–Piraeus–occasionally Limassol and Haifa; westbound include Halifax instead of Boston. Caribbean and Mediterranean cruises in winter.
Particulars: 21,716 gross tons; 640 × 85 × 29 feet.
Builders: Fairfield Shipbuilding & Engineering Co., Glasgow, Scotland, 1956.
Machinery: Steam turbines; twin screw; service speed 21 knots.
Capacity: 109 first class and 1,145 tourist class; 900 one-class for cruising.

Maiden arrival for the *Olympia* off Lower Manhattan in October 1953. (*Gillespie-Faber collection*)

1956–64: Sailed as *Empress of Britain*, Canadian Pacific Steamships, British flag.
February 1964: Purchased by Trans-Oceanic Navigation Co. (Greek Line).
November 1964: Delivered to Greek Line, Greek flag.
1964–65: Major refit at Genoa; passenger capacity increased from 1,054 to 1,254; tonnage relisted from 25,516 to 21,716.
March 1965: Renamed *Queen Anna Maria* by HM Queen Anne Marie of Greece.
March 24, 1965: Departed Piraeus on maiden voyage to New York.
February 19, 1967: Grounded off Kingston, Jamaica during cruise; refloated on February 26.
1970: Cruising only.
January 11, 1975: Left New York empty to escape creditors; ending Greek Line passenger service; arrived Piraeus on January 22 and laid-up; later offered for sale.
December 1975: Sold to Carnival Cruise Lines, Panamanian flag, renamed *Carnivale*.
January 1976: Refitted; capacity listed as 1,198.
February 1976: Maiden cruise: seven-day Miami-Caribbean.
1988: Capacity listed as 1,187.
June 1990: Registered in the Bahamas.
1993: Transferred to Fiesta Marina Cruises (Carnival Corp), Bahamian flag; renamed *Fiesta Marina*; unsuccessful.
May 1994: Sold to Epirotiki Lines, Greek flag; renamed *Olympic*. Eastern Mediterranean cruises mostly.
1996: Transferred to Royal Olympic Cruises, Greek flag.
1997: Operated on charter by Thomson Cruises; renamed *The Topaz*.
1998: Sold to Topaz International Shipping Co., Panamanian flag. Capacity relisted as 1,050.
June 2003: Began charter as Japanese-operated *Peace Boat*.
April 2008: Ended charter as *Peace Boat*; later sold for scrap.
July 4, 2008: Arrived at Alang to be scrapped.

Above: Busy Day at New York in September 1957. *From top to bottom*: the *Britannic*, the *Queen Mary*, the *Mauretania*, the *Flandre*, the *Olympia*, the *United States*, and the *Independence*. (*Port Authority of New York & New Jersey*)

Right: The former *Queen Anna Maria*, but in her later years as the cruise ship *Olympic*. (*Luis Miguel Correia*)

Below: Summer's Day at New York in 1990. *From left to right:* the *Fantasy*, the *Royal Odyssey*, the *Golden Odyssey*, the *Regal Empress*, the *Song of America*, and the *Meridian*. (*Moran Towing & Transportation Co*)

20

Grimaldi-Siosa Lines

Ascania (1926)

Service: 1957–60: Periodic transatlantic sailings Southampton –Le Havre–New York or Quebec City.
Particulars: 9,536 gross tons; 490 × 60 × 24 feet.
Builders: Ateliers et Chantiers de la Loire, Saint-Nazaire, France, 1926.
Machinery: Steam turbines; twin screw; service speed 16 knots.
Capacity: Eighty-seven first class and 1,160 tourist class.

1926: Completed as *Florida* for Transports Maritimes, French flag; Marseilles–Rio de Janeiro–Buenos Aires service.
April 1, 1931: Badly damaged off Gibraltar in collision with aircraft carrier *HMS Glorious*; later repaired.
1940: Wartime troopship service.
November 13, 1942: Sunk by Nazi bombers at Bone, Algeria.
May 1944: Refloated then towed to Toulon for repairs; second funnel removed.
1945: Resumed South American sailings from Marseilles.
1955: Sold to Grimaldi-Siosa Lines, Italian flag; renamed *Ascania*; refitted.
1955–56: Chartered to French Government for trooping: Algeria, Southeast Asia, etc.
May 1957: Began seasonal Le Havre–Quebec City sailings.
1959: Further sailings to Quebec City.
1960: Some Plymouth–New York sailings.
1960–67: Southampton–Spain–West Indies migrant and low-fare service; later seven-day western Mediterranean cruises from Genoa.
October 1, 1967: Laid-up at La Spezia, Italy.
April 1968: Scrapped.

Irpinia

Service: 1959–61: Genoa–Naples–Palermo–Gibraltar–Azores–Quebec City–Montreal service; 1956–59: occasional voyages to New York as well.
Particulars: 12,279 gross tons; 537 × 67 × 23 feet.
Builders: Swan, Hunter & Wigham Richardson Shipbuilders Ltd., Newcastle, England, 1929.
Machinery: Steam turbines; twin screw; service speed 16 knots.
Capacity: 187 first class and 1,034 tourist class.

1929: Launched as *Campana* for Transports Maritimes, French flag.
December 1929: Entered Marseilles–Rio de Janeiro–Buenos Aires service.
June 1940: Laid-up at Buenos Aires for wartime safety.
July 1943: Seized by Argentine Government; renamed *Rio Jachal*; made some wartime voyages including Buenos Aires–New Orleans.
1946: Returned to French owners; name reverted to *Campana*; resumed Marseilles–South America service (and also some sailings to Southeast Asia).
June 1955: Sold to Grimaldi-Siosa Lines, Italian flag; renamed *Irpinia*. Major refit: new raked bow that increased length from 527 to 537 feet; tonnage listed as 12,279; later entered Genoa–West Indies service.
September 1956: First Southampton–New York sailing.
April 1959: Commenced Mediterranean–Canada sailings.
1962: Major refit at Trieste; new Fiat diesels fitted; two funnels replaced one; now 13,204 gross tons; 187 first class and 1,034 tourist class, Later resumed Genoa–West Indies service.
March 1970: Cruising only, mostly seven-day Mediterranean cruises from Genoa.
June 1975: Summer Scandinavian cruises from Tilbury.
1976: Used as a floating prop in film *Voyage of the Damned*.
1976–81: Further cruising from Genoa.
1981: Laid-up at La Spezia.
September 5, 1983: Sold to Cantieri Navali Santa Maria; scrapped at La Spezia.

The classic-looking *Irpinia* was later rebuilt with a single, tapered funnel. (*Author's collection*)

Caribbean Bound: The *Ascania* at Southampton. (*Mick Lindsay collection*)

21

Hamburg-Atlantic Line

Hanseatic (1930)

Service: Cuxhaven (Hamburg)–Southampton–Cherbourg–New York. Winter cruising from New York, Port Everglades, and Cuxhaven.
Particulars: 30,029 gross tons; 672 × 83 × 31 feet.
Builders: Fairfield Shipbuilding & Engineering Co., Glasgow, Scotland, 1930.
Machinery: Steam turbines; twin screw; service speed 21 knots.
Capacity: Eighty-five first class and 1,167 tourist class.

1930–42: Sailed as *Empress of Japan*, Canadian Pacific Steamships Ltd., British flag.
1942–57: Sailed as *Empress of Scotland*, Canadian Pacific Steamships Ltd., British flag (qv).
1958 Jan: Acquired by Hamburg-Atlantic Line, West German flag; provisionally renamed *Scotland* and then *Hanseatic*. Bought for $2.8 million; rebuilt at Howaldtswerke Shipyard, Hamburg, for $3.2 million. Three funnels replaced by two; accommodation modernized and increased from 708 to 1,252 passengers; new bow fitted increasing length from 666 to 672 feet; tonnage increased from 26,313 to 30,029.
July 1958: Maiden voyage from Cuxhaven to New York.
1961: Extended tops added to funnels.
September 7, 1966: Seriously damaged by fire at New York's Pier 84; laid-up in Brooklyn shipyard for inspection, but beyond economic repair. Sold to Eisen und Metall A/G; towed to Hamburg; and scrapped.

Rebuilt from the three-funnel *Empress of Scotland*, the *Hanseatic* makes her debut at Hamburg in July 1958. (*ALF collection*)

22

Holland-America Line

Volendam

Service: 1947–51: Rotterdam–New York austerity sailings.
Particulars: 15,434 gross tons; 579 × 67 feet.
Builders: Harland & Wolff Ltd., Belfast, Northern Ireland, 1922.
Machinery: Steam turbines; geared to quadruple screw; service speed 15 knots.
Capacity: 1,693 one-class passengers.

July 6, 1922: Launched.
November 4, 1922: Departed from Rotterdam on maiden voyage to New York via Boulogne and Plymouth.
1940: Begin Allied trooping.
May 1940: Temporarily housed parts of exiled Dutch Government at Falmouth.
August 30, 1940: Torpedoed 300 miles off Ireland; later taken in tow and beached; eventually repaired at Birkenhead.
July 1941: Resumed trooping.
July 1945: Returned to Rotterdam; given partial refit; chartered to British Government for further trooping.
1946: Dutch Government trooping and evacuation services to/from Indonesia; also migrant sailings Rotterdam–Australia.
1947: Further refit but never fully restored; began seasonal sailings between Rotterdam and New York.
November 1951: Sold for scrap at Rotterdam.
February 1952: Demolition began.

Veendam

Service: Rotterdam–Le Havre–Southampton–New York; winter cruising.
Particulars: 15,652 gross tons; 579 × 67 feet.
Builders: Harland & Wolff Ltd., Belfast, Northern Ireland, 1923.
Machinery: Steam turbines; geared to quadruple screw; service speed 15 knots.
Capacity: 223 first class and 363 tourist class.

November 18, 1922: Launched.
April 18, 1923: Left Rotterdam on maiden voyage to New York via Boulogne and Plymouth.
1930: Chartered to Furness–Bermuda Line for New York–Bermuda service; then returned to Holland-America.
May 1940: Caught at Rotterdam during Nazi invasion; later taken to Gdynia for use as a submarine tender and recreation ship for U-boat crews.
May 1945: Found by Allied invasion forces at Hamburg.
October 1945: Towed to Rotterdam; major overhaul and restoration; accommodation restyled for 223 first class and 363 tourist class.
January 1947: Resumed Rotterdam–New York sailings.
October 30, 1953: Final sailing from Rotterdam to New York.
December 1953: Sold to Bethlehem Steel Co. for scrapping at Baltimore.

Edam

Service: 1949–53: Rotterdam–New York and other U.S. East Coast ports (Philadelphia, Baltimore, Boston, etc.).
Particulars: 8,871grt; 462 × 55 × 29 feet.
Builders: De Schelde Shipyard, Flushing, Holland, 1921.
Machinery: Steam turbines; single screw; service speed 14 knots.
Capacity: Ninety one-class passengers.

March 18, 1920: Laid down for Holland-America Line, Dutch flag.
January 15, 1921: Launched.
September 1921: Maiden voyage from Rotterdam via Vigo to Havana and Gulf of Mexico ports. Fourteen first class, 174 second and 800 third class passengers.
1928: Accommodation changed to fourteen first class and 950 third class.

January 1932: Laid-up owing to the Depression.
1934: Rebuilt at Rotterdam; original twin funnels reduced to one; accommodation reduced to thirty first class and sixty third class.
1935: Rotterdam–New York service.
June 1940–March 1946: Operated by British Ministry of Transport, managed by Furness Withy & Co.
February 10, 1940: Rescued survivors from Holland-America freighter *Burgerdijk*.
May 1940: Collision in River Mersey with Norwegian freighter *Taranger*.
1946: Returned to Holland-America Line; Rotterdam–U.S. East Coast ports service.
1949: Refitted; ninety first class passengers; Rotterdam–New York service.
August 1953: Scrapped at Rotterdam.

Leerdam

Service: 1946–53: Rotterdam–New York and other U.S. East Coast ports (see *Edam*).
Particulars: 8,871 gross tons; 462 × 55 × 29 feet.
Builders: New Waterway Shipbuilding Co., Schiedam, Holland, 1920
Machinery: Steam turbines; single screw; service speed 13 knots.
Capacity: Ninety-eight one-class passengers.
June 30, 1919: Laid-down for Holland-America Line, Dutch flag.
December 6, 1920: Launched.
October 25, 1921: Maiden voyage from Rotterdam via Vigo to Havana and U.S. Gulf Coast ports. Fourteen first class, 174 second class and 800 third class.
1928: Refitted: fourteen first class and 950 third class.
1934: Refitted at Rotterdam; two funnels replaced by one; accommodation reduced to thirty first class and sixty third class; thereafter, Rotterdam–New York service.
June 1940–June 1945: Chartered to British Ministry of War Transport. Mostly North Atlantic convoy service.
January 1943: Narrowly averted major explosion when loaded with explosives in New York harbor and nearly rammed by freighter *Extavia* (American Export Lines).
December 1943: Began around-the-world voyage of 134 days.
September 1945: Began Rotterdam–Baltimore service
1946: Refitted: ninety-eight all-first class passengers.
December 1952: Laid-up at Rotterdam.
August 1953: Arrived in Yokohama to be scrapped.

Dongedyk

Service: Service: Bremen–Hamburg–Antwerp–Rotterdam–London–Bermuda–Curaçao–Cristobal–Los Angeles–San Francisco–Portland–Seattle–Victoria–Vancouver; occasional calls at San Diego, Eureka, Astoria, Tacoma, etc.
Particulars: 10,942 gross tons; 529 × 61 × 36 feet.
Builders: Wilton's Engineering & Slipway Co., Rotterdam, Holland, 1929.
Machinery: B&W type diesels; twin screw; service speed 15 knots.
Capacity: Fifty-two one-class passengers.

October 1930: Entered Rotterdam–North American West Coast service via Panama as *Delftdijk*, Holland-America Line, Dutch flag.
May 5, 1940: Escaped from Rotterdam prior to Nazi attack and invasion.

The *Leerdam* was pressed into New York service following World War II. (*Gillespie-Faber collection*)

The *Dongedyk* passing Tilbury in August 1956. (*Mick Lindsay collection*)

1941: Attacked by Nazi bomber while lying at Peterhead; later taken to Newcastle for repairs, but then damaged in an air raid. Out of service for one year.
1946: Refitted and resumed sailing.
January 24, 1950: Struck an undetonated mine in River Elbe; taken to Schiedam for extensive repairs; re-engined with MAN-type diesels; service speed increased to 16 knots; fifty-two passengers.
1952: Renamed *Dongedyk;* resumed sailings.
1966: Sold to Chung Lien Navigation Co. for $400,000; renamed *Tung Long*; resold for scrapping.
September 12, 1966: Arrived at Kaohsiung and scrapped.

Dalerdyk

Service: Northern Europe–North American West Coast via Panama (same ports as *Dongedyk*).
Particulars: 10,820 gross tons; 509 × 65 × 30 feet.
Builders: Wilton's Engineering & Slipway Co., Rotterdam, Holland, 1930.
Machinery: Sulzer diesels; twin screw; 14½ knots service speed.
Capacity: Forty-six all-first class passengers.

May 17, 1930: Launched as *Damsterdijk* Holland-America Line, Dutch flag.
September 9, 1930: Left Rotterdam on maiden voyage to North American Pacific Coast.
May 1940: Seized at Rotterdam by invading Nazi forces.
August 1940: Painted entirely in black and prepared for use in intended Nazi invasion of Britain.
1941: Managed by Hamburg-America Line; used as a target ship by Nazi aircraft.
1943: Used for target practice by Nazi U-boats in the Baltic; renamed *Mülhausen.*
April–May 1945: Damaged by Allied air attacks of German ports.
February 1946: Returned in badly damaged condition to Holland–America.
1946–49: Repaired at Schiedam; re-engined with Sulzer diesels; modern accommodation for forty-six passengers; later renamed *Dalerdyk.*
February 1949: Resumed Rotterdam–North American West Coast service.
1963: Sold to Belvientos Compañía de Navigación, Panamanian flag; renamed *Presvia*; then resold to Japanese shipbreakers.

Duivendyk

Service: Northern Europe–North American West Coast via Panama (same ports as *Dongedyk*).
Particulars: 8,338 gross tons; 499 × 63 × 32 feet.
Builders: Deutsche Werft, Hamburg, Germany, 1930.
Machinery: Steam turbines; geared to single screw; service speed 14 knots.
Capacity: Forty-five first class passengers

1930: Completed as *Vancouver*, Hamburg-America Line, German flag; North Europe–North American West Coast service.
May 10, 1940: Seized by Dutch forces at Curaçao; renamed *Curacao;* used as Allied transport.
1946: Allocated to Holland-America Line; renamed *Duivendijk*; refitted and restored; Rotterdam–North American Pacific coast service.
1953: Named restyled as *Duivendyk.*
October 1959: Scrapped in Japan.

Nieuw Amsterdam

Service: Rotterdam–Le Havre–Southampton–New York; winter cruising from New York to the Caribbean mostly.
Particulars: 36,667 gross tons; 758 × 88 × 31 feet.
Builders: Rotterdam Dry Dock Co., Rotterdam, Holland, 1938.
Machinery: Steam turbines; geared to twin screw; service speed 21 knots.
Capacity: 552 first class, 426 cabin class, and 209 tourist passengers.
Notes: Holland's flagship and largest liner 1938–59. One of the most popular and beloved of all Atlantic liners.

January 1936: Keel laid; intended to be named *Prinsendam*.
April 10, 1937: Launched by HM Queen Wilhelmina as *Nieuw Amsterdam*.
May 16, 1938: Maiden arrival at New York from Rotterdam.
September 1939: Began cruising from New York to Bermuda and the Caribbean for safety from war in Europe.
May 1940: Laid-up at Hoboken, New Jersey pier.
September 1940: Transferred to British Ministry of War Transport for trooping; refitted at Halifax.

The beautiful *Nieuw Amsterdam* at Hoboken in the early 1950s. (*Port Authority of New York & New Jersey*)

April 26, 1946: Returned to Rotterdam and fondly dubbed "Darling of the Dutch"; decommissioned from military service with a war record of 378,361 passengers and 530,432 steaming miles.
1946–47: Major refit.
October 29, 1947: Arrived at New York on first post-war crossing from Rotterdam.
1956–57: Major refit; repainted with grey hull.
1961: Refit: Accommodation restyled as 574 first class and 583 tourist class; tonnage relisted as 36,982.
January 1965: Rammed and sank a barge in New York harbor.
July 1967: Inspection revealed worn-out boilers; rumored that ship would be withdrawn scrapped.
September 1967: Refitted instead with boilers acquired from U.S. Navy, shipped to Holland and installed at Schiedam shipyard.
September 1971: Ended Holland-America's trans-Atlantic service; commenced two-month refit.
November 1971: Based at Port Everglades for year-round Caribbean cruising.
1972: Registered at Willemstad, Curaçao instead of Rotterdam.
December 1973: Final cruise.
March 2, 1974: Arrived at Kaohsiung for scrapping.

Noordam

Service: Rotterdam–New York direct.
Particulars: 10,726 gross tons; 501 × 64 × 30 feet.
Builders: P. Smit Jr. Shipbuilders, Rotterdam, Holland, 1938.
Machinery: B&W type diesels; geared to twin screw; service speed 17 knots.
Capacity: 148 first class passengers.

April 9, 1938: Launched.
September 28, 1938: Departed Rotterdam on maiden voyage to New York.
March 1940: Owing to war in Europe, ship transferred to New York–Dutch East Indies service.
April 1942: Taken over by U.S. War Shipping Board; used as a transport.
July 1946: Resumed Rotterdam–New York service.
May 1963: Withdrawn from Holland–America service; later sold to Cielomar S/A, Panamanian flag; chartered to Messageries Maritimes for their Marseilles–Panama–South Pacific–Australia service; to have been renamed *Wallisien*, but renamed *Oceanien* instead.
February 17, 1967: Arrived at Split, Yugoslavia, to be scrapped by Brodospas.

The *Nieuw Amsterdam* during a cruise visit to Copenhagen. (*ALF collection*)

One of the finest combination passenger-cargo ships, the *Noordam* made only direct crossings between Rotterdam and New York. (*Holland-America Line*)

Westerdam

Service: Rotterdam–New York direct service.
Particulars: 12,149 gross tons; 518 × 66 × 31 feet.
Builders: Wilton-Fijenoord Shipyard, Schiedam, Holland, 1940–46.
Machinery: MAN-type diesels; geared to twin screw; service speed 16 knots.
Capacity: 134 first class passengers.

1938: Ordered; intended for North Europe–North America West Coast service.
July 27, 1940: Floated.
August 27, 1940: Incomplete ship sunk in Allied air raid; later refloated.
September 1944: Deliberately sunk by Dutch Underground to avoid use by Nazi occupation forces; refloated by Nazis and then sun again by Underground.
September 13, 1945: Refloated and refitted; finally completed.
June 1946: Maiden voyage from Rotterdam to New York; first Holland-America passenger ship in post-war service.
November 21, 1964: Withdrawn from service at Rotterdam.
January 1965: Reported that she would become floating hostel for workers at the Royal Netherlands Blast Furnaces & Foundries plant similar to *Arosa Sun* (qv); never materialized.
February 1965: Sold for scrapping at Alicante, Spain.

Diemerdyk

Service: Northern Europe–North American West Coast via Panama (same ports as *Dongedyk*).
Particulars: 11,195 gross tons; 494 × 64 × 30 feet.
Builders: Wilton-Fijenoord Shipyard, Schiedam, Holland, 1950.
Machinery: Steam turbines; twin screw; service speed 16½ knots.
Capacity: Sixty-one all-first class passengers.

1949: Intended for affiliate Red Star Line service: Antwerp–New York. Plans later changed and ship assigned to North American West Coast service.
June 1950: Completed; Rotterdam–New York voyage and then assigned to Pacific Coast service.
1968: Sold Orient Africa Line (C. Y. Tung), Liberian flag; operated by Orient Overseas Line in around-the-world service; renamed *Oriental Amiga.*
December 1, 1968: First sailing as *Oriental Amiga*.
1974: Transferred to Chinese Maritime Trust, Taiwanese flag; freighter only service thereafter.
June 30, 1979: Arrived at Kaohsiung and broken-up by Chi Young Steel Enterprises.

Ryndam/Waterman (1951)

Service: Rotterdam–Le Havre–Southampton–Cobh–New York (until 1959) and to Montreal (beginning in 1960). Also cruising.
Particulars: 15,015 gross tons; 503 × 69 × 28 feet.
Builders: Wilton-Fijenoord Shipyard, Schiedam, Holland, 1951.
Machinery: Steam turbines; geared to twin screw; service speed 16½ knots.
Capacity: Thirty-nine first class and 836 tourist class passengers; 550 one-class on cruises.

Dressed in flags, the *Ryndam* leaves Dutch waters in this late '60s view. (*Mick Lindsay collection*)

1949: Intended to be sixty-passenger combination ship *Dinteldyk*; construction using surplus U.S. Navy steam turbines dating from 1945.
October 30, 1950: Decision announced to re-design *Dinteldyk* as full passenger liner and instead to be named *Ryndam.*
July 1951: Maiden voyage from Rotterdam to New York. First Holland-America liner with grey hull; tourist class dominance; inexpensive $20-a-day fares to/from Europe. She and sister *Maasdam* were great successes; averaged 85 percent capacity on crossings in 1950s and 96 percent on cruises.
July 1958: Began regular eastbound calls at Galway.
March 1960: Began service to Canada, to Quebec City and Montreal; winter sailings to Halifax and sometimes Boston.
July 1960: First cruise from Montreal—to Saguenay, Gaspe, Bermuda, New York, and Quebec City.
1961: Refit and some tourist class cabins fitted with private bathrooms.
November 7, 1964: Left Rotterdam an experimental voyage to Southampton, Suez, Fremantle, Melbourne, Sydney, Wellington, Papeete, Los Angles, Panama Canal, Kingston, Southampton, and return to Rotterdam.
1965: Refit at Bremerhaven.
February 1966: Transferred to Europe–Canada Line, West German flag; German officers and crew, but delivery made in Sep 1966.
August 1966: Final Holland–America sailing to Canada.
October 1966: Departed on first Europe–Canada Line voyage, but chartered to Chapman College of Orange, California for around-the-world "floating university" cruise.
September 1967: Transferred to Trans-Ocean Steamship Co., Dutch flag; Dutch officers and crew. Further student voyages and "floating university" cruises.
May 24, 1968: Renamed *Waterman* while berthed at Pier 40, New York.
October 10, 1968: Reverted to Holland-America Line; renamed *Ryndam.*
1969: Four Le Havre–Southampton–New York voyages plus two world voyages.
1970: Two Boston–Cherbourg–Southampton voyages plus two world voyages
October 9, 1970: First Indonesian stewards and dining room staff for Holland-America introduced onboard.
June 1971: Laid-up at Schiedam. Reportedly sold to Sovereign Cruises, Maltese flag, for fly'n sail Mediterranean cruising; never materialized.
August 1972: Sold to Worldwide Cruises S/A (Epirotiki Lines), Greek flag, for $2½ million. Extensively rebuilt as *Atlas* for Eastern Mediterranean cruising.
1988: Sold to Pride Cruise Lines, U.S. flag; *renamed Pride of Mississippi.*
December 1988: Began gambling cruises from Gulfport, Mississippi.
1991: Renamed *Pride of Galveston* (*Pride of Texas* had been considered).
1993: Renamed *Copa Casino*; used as moored casino-restaurant ship.
2002: Laid-up at Mobile.
March 3, 2003: Left Mobile under tow for Alang to be scrapped.
March 16, 2003 16 Mar: Sank off Dominican Republic.

The *Maasdam* seen along the New Waterway. (*Mick Lindsay collection*)

Maasdam

Service: Rotterdam–Le Havre–Southampton–Cobh–New York; later (1963) extended to Bremerhaven. Occasional cruising.
Particulars: 15,024 gross tons; 503 × 69 × 28 feet.
Builders: Wilton-Fijenoord Shipyard, Schiedam, Holland, 1930.
Machinery: Steam turbines; geared to twin screw; service speed 16½ knots.
Capacity: Thirty-nine first class and 836 tourist class passengers; 550 one-class on cruises.

December 19, 1950: Keel laid; intended to be sixty-passenger combination passenger-cargo ship *Diemerdyk* for North Europe–North American Pacific Coast service; later redesigned as full passenger ship.
April 5, 1951: Launched.
August 1952: Maiden voyage Rotterdam–Le Havre–Southampton–Montreal–New York. Largest liner to date to use the Cape Cod Canal.
December 10, 1952: Rammed and sank German tanker *Ellen* in fog in the New Waterway; six crewmen lost.
October 3, 1954: Collided with French freighter *Tofevo* off Rhode Island; *Maasdam* returned to New York for repairs.
1955: First Holland-America liner to be fitted with stabilizers.
1955: Rammed dockside at Wilhelminakade, Rotterdam.
December 22, 1962: Arrived in New York two days late, coated in ice and after encountering 35-foot waves, snow, ice, sleet, and 75-mph winds. Arrived with 200 passengers and 18,000 sacks of Christmas mail.
February 15, 1963: Heavily damaged after striking two wrecks in River Weser near Bremerhaven.
October 1966: Transferred to Rotterdam-Montreal service to replace *Ryndam*.
May 15, 1968: Sold to Polish Ocean Lines; with delivery late Sep; renamed *Stefan Batory* (qv).

Statendam

Service: Rotterdam–Le Havre–Southampton–New York; off-season cruising.
Particulars: 24,294 gross tons; 642 × 81 × 26 feet.
Builders: Wilton-Fijenoord Shipyard, Schiedam, Holland, 1957.
Machinery: Steam turbines; geared to twin screw; service speed 19 knots.

June 2, 1956: Floated in dry dock, not launched.
December 15, 1956: Broke down during sea trials; towed back to Schiedam.
January 23, 1957: Named by HRH Crown Princess Beatrix during short voyage in North Sea.
February 6, 1957: Departed Rotterdam on maiden voyage to New York.
1966: Cruising only; later including cruises from San Francisco and Los Angeles.
September 1971–February 1972: Given $7 million refit and made more suitable for cruising; 740 one-class passengers; first Holland-America liner repainted with dark blue hull.
1973: Registry transferred from Rotterdam to Willemstad, Curaçao.

The Hoboken Piers in September 1957: The American Export Lines' freighter piers at the bottom; then the *Statendam*, *Noordam*, and *Maasdam* at the Holland-America piers; and the *Groote Beer* beyond. (*Moran Towing & Transportation Co.*)

1974: Assigned to New York–Bermuda service; winter cruising from Port Everglades.
1974–82: Periodic mechanical troubles.
May 1981: Reassigned to seasonal service from Vancouver to Alaska; continued winter cruising from Florida.
October 1982: Sold to Artus Investment Inc., Panamanian flag for use by Paquet Cruises; renamed *Rhapsody*.
March 28, 1984: Grounded near Georgetown, Grand Cayman; badly damaged.
June 15, 1984: Refloated and towed to Galveston for repairs.
September 1984: Resumed cruising.
May 1986: Sold to Lelakis Group, Panamanian flag; renamed *Regent Star* for use by Regency Cruises; converted to diesel propulsion.
July 1987: Resumed cruises.
1990: Transferred to Bahamian registry.
July 1995: Engine breakdown during Alaskan cruise; passengers transferred to the nearby *Rotterdam*.
November 1995: At Piraeus for lengthy repairs.
1996: Following collapse of Regency Cruises, ship seized for debt.
October 1996: Auctioned off to Royal Venture Cruise Lines, to become *Star Venture*; never materialized.
1997: Ship to become *Sea Harmony* for time-share cruising; never materialized.
October 1997: Arrested for further debts.
2004: Sold to Indian scrappers; renamed *Harmony I*.
April 28, 2004: Arrived under tow at Alang; later scrapped.

Dinteldyk

Service: Northern Europe–North American West Coast via Panama (same ports as *Dongedyk*).
Particulars: 11,366 gross tons; 504 × 69 × 30 feet.
Builders: Wilton-Fijenoord Shipyard, Schiedam, Holland, 1957.
Machinery: Steam turbines; twin screw; service speed 16½ knots.
Capacity: Sixty all-first class passengers.
March 1957: Maiden voyage from North Europe to North American West Coast.
1970: Sold to Oriental Central America Lines (C. Y. Tung Group), Liberian flag; renamed *Oriental Fantasia*; around-the-world passenger-cargo service.
1973: Transferred to Pacific Union Lines (C. Y. Tung Group), Hong Kong; renamed *Hong Kong Success*; freighter service only hereafter and refitted to carry containers.
1978: Transferred back to Oriental Central America Lines (C. Y. Tung Group). Hong Kong.
December 28, 1978: Departed from Kobe for Kaohsiung; sold to Chien Tai Iron Works.
January 1, 1979: Arrived Kaohsiung and then scrapped.

Rotterdam

Service: Rotterdam–Le Havre–Southampton–New York; off-season cruising.
Particulars: 38,645 gross tons; 748 × 94 × 29 feet.
Builders: Rotterdam Dry-dock Co., Rotterdam, Holland, 1959.

Above: The *Diemerdyk* departs from Holland-America's Rotterdam terminal. (*ALF collection*)

Right: In her very last days, the former *Statendam* made a sad sight. (*Philippe Brebant collection*)

The *Oriental Fantasia* (the former *Dinteldyk*) seen at Hong Kong. (*Alex Duncan*)

The beautiful *Rotterdam* departing from Southampton. (*Mick Lindsay collection*)

Machinery: Steam turbines; geared to twin screw; service speed 20½ knots.
Capacity: Variable: 580/301 first class passengers and 809/1,055 tourist class; 730 one-class for cruising.

December 14, 1956: Laid down.
September 13, 1958: Launched by HM Queen Juliana; cost £13 million.
September 3, 1959: Left Rotterdam on maiden voyage to New York.
1969: Cruising only.
1973: Transferred registry from Rotterdam to Curaçao.
September 1973: Repainted with dark blue hull.
April 1981: Reassigned to seasonal service (April–October) from Vancouver to Alaska; cruising to the Caribbean at other times and annual world cruise from New York.
1983: Tonnage relisted as 38,644; 1,100 cruise passengers.
1989: Holland-America bought by Carnival Corporation.
October 1997: Sold to Premier Cruises, Bahamian flag; renamed *Rembrandt.*
September 15, 2000: Arrested for debt at Halifax following collapse of Premier Cruises.
December 30, 2000: Laid-up at Freeport pending resale; rumored to be scrapped.
2004: Sold to Dutch buyers for preservation and further use as hotel, museum, etc. at Rotterdam.
July 12, 2004: Arrived under tow at Gibraltar for asbestos removal and other preliminary work; later further repairs and restoration at Cadiz and then to Poland and Germany. August 8, 2008: Returned to Rotterdam.
February 15, 2010: Opened as hotel, museum, entertainment center, training school, etc.
2012: Rumored to have financial troubles and to be sold to Middle Eastern buyers; never materialized.
January 12, 2013: Sold to WestCord Hotels Inc.; remains at Rotterdam.

Prinses Margriet

Service: 1963–67: Rotterdam–New York direct.
Particulars: 9,336 gross tons; 456 × 61 × 28 feet.
Builders: De Merwede Shipbuilding Yard, Hardinxveld, Holland, 1961.
Machinery: MAN-type diesel; single screw; service speed 17 knots.
Capacity: 111 one-class passengers.

1961–64: Sailed as *Prinses Margriet* for Oranje Line, Dutch flag (qv).
April 1964: Chartered to Holland-America Line for Rotterdam–New York service.
December 1964: Sold to Holland-America Line, Dutch flag; Rotterdam–New York service.
December 15, 1967: First sailing from New York on charter to Royal Netherlands Steamship Co. for twelve-day voyages to the Caribbean.
June 3, 1970: Ended New York–Caribbean service.
1970: Sold to Nauru Local Government Council, Nauru flag; renamed *Enna G*; San Francisco-Pacific service.
1984: Laid-up; later used as moored hotel in the Marshall Islands.
1990: Scrapped in Thailand.

The *Prinses Margriet* in Holland-America colors as she departs from Rotterdam, bound for New York. (*Mick Lindsay collection*)

23

Home Lines

Brasil/Homeland

Service: 1950–51: Genoa–Naples–Palermo–Gibraltar–Halifax (westbound only)–New York; 1951–55: Hamburg–Southampton–Cherbourg–Halifax (westbound only)–New York.
Particulars: 10,043 gross tons; 538 × 60 feet.
Builders: Alexander & Stephen & Sons Ltd., Glasgow, Scotland, 1905.
Machinery: Steam turbines; twin screw; service speed 18 knots.
Capacity: Ninety-six first class and 846 tourist class.
Notes: Reached fiftieth year.

1905–20: Sailed as *Virginian*; first for Allan Line, British flag; then Canadian Pacific Steamships, also British flag.
1920–48: Sailed as *Drottningholm* for Swedish American Line, Swedish flag.
March 1946: Sold to Home Lines, Panamanian flag; delivery postponed until 1948.
1948: Transferred to Home Lines; renamed *Brasil.*
July 1948: Began Genoa–South America sailings.
April 1950: Commenced Genoa–Naples–New York service.
1951: Major refit; renamed *Homeland*; tonnage relisted from 10,249 to 10,043. Commenced Hamburg–New York sailings.
1952: Resumed Genoa–Naples–New York service.
March 1955: Scrapped at Trieste.

Argentina

Service: During 1952: Genoa–Naples–Palermo–Gibraltar–Halifax (westbound only)–New York.
Particulars: 11,015 gross tons; 530 × 61 feet.
Builders: Cammell Laird & Co. Ltd., Birkenhead, England, 1913.
Machinery: Steam turbines; twin screw; service speed 15 knots.
Capacity: Thirty-two first class and 969 tourist class.

A fine painting of the elderly *Argentina* at New York's Pier 88 by the late artist Joe Wilhelm. (*Author's collection*)

April 8, 1913: Launched.
September 1913: Maiden voyage Oslo–Bergen–New York as *Bergensfjord* for Norwegian America Line; 10,666 gross tons; 105 first class, 216 second class and 759 third class.
1920: Converted from coal to oil burner.
1931: Major refit at Bremen: new turbines fitted; passenger accommodation restyled as 367 cabin class and 572 third class.
1938: Accommodation again restyled: ninety cabin class, 155 tourist class and 500 third class.
April 15, 1940: Laid-up at New York owing to war in Europe.
November 1940: Allied troopship: British management with Norwegian crew.
February 1946: Returned to Norwegian America Line.

November 1946: Sold to Home Lines, Panamanian flag; renamed *Argentina*; refitted.
January 13, 1947: First sailing Genoa–Rio de Janeiro–Buenos Aires.
September 1949: Transferred to Genoa–Caribbean service.
April 1952: Began Genoa–Naples–New York service.
February 1953: Sold to Zim Lines, Israeli flag; renamed *Jerusalem* (qv).

Atlantic (1927)

Service: 1949–51: Genoa–Naples–Palermo–Gibraltar–Halifax (westbound only)–New York; 1952–54: Southampton–Le Havre–Quebec City. Winter cruising.
Particulars: 20,553 gross tons; 582 × 83 × 29 feet.
Builders: William Cramp & Sons Ship & Engine Building Co., Philadelphia, Pennsylvania, 1927.
Machinery: Steam turbines; twin screw; service speed 21 knots.
Capacity: 349 first class, 203 cabin class, and 626 tourist class.

June 26, 1926: Launched as *Malolo,* Matson Navigation Co., U.S. flag.
May 25, 1927: During trials, collided with Norwegian freighter *Jakob Christensen* off Nantucket. *Malolo* stayed afloat despite being flooded with 7,000 tons of sea water; later repaired at Brooklyn.
November 1927: Entered San Francisco–Honolulu service; 693 all-first class passengers.
1937: Major refit; renamed *Matsonia.*
February 1942: Became U.S. Navy troopship.
April 1946: Decommissioned from troopship service; later resumed San Francisco–Honolulu service.
1948: Sold to Home Lines, Panamanian flag; renamed *Atlantic.* Refitted with expanded accommodation.
May 14, 1949: Departed from Genoa for New York.
February 1952: Commenced Southampton–Quebec City service.
December 1954: Transferred to National Hellenic American Line, Greek flag; renamed *Queen Frederica* (qv).

Italia

Service: 1949–51: Genoa–Naples–Palermo–Gibraltar–Halifax (westbound only)–New York; 1952–58: Cuxhaven (Hamburg)–Southampton–Le Havre–Halifax (westbound only)–New York; 1959–60: Cuxhaven (Hamburg)–Southampton–Le Havre–Quebec City–Montreal. Winter cruising from New York to the Caribbean and Mediterranean.
Particulars: 21,532 gross tons; 609 × 78 × 20 feet.
Builders: Blohm & Voss A/G, Hamburg, Germany, 1928.
Machinery: B&W type diesels; twin screw; service speed 17 knots.
Capacity: 213 first class and 1,106 tourist class.

March 7, 1928: Launched.
November 24, 1928: Left Gothenburg for New York on maiden voyage as *Kungsholm*, Swedish American Line, Swedish flag. Cruising also.
1932–33: Refit; repainted with white hull.
January 1942: Sold to War Shipping Administration, U.S. flag; renamed *John Ericsson*; trooping. Managed by United States Lines.
March 1947: Damaged by fire at Pier 90, New York.
July 1947: Resold to Swedish American Line, Swedish flag.
December 1947: Sold to Home Lines, Panamanian flag; renamed *Italia*; refitted at Genoa.
July 27, 1948: Departed Genoa on maiden voyage to Rio de Janeiro and Buenos Aires.
June 12, 1949: Left Genoa on first crossing to New York.
March 1952: Commenced Hamburg–New York sailings.
October 6, 1954: Rammed and sank tug *Fairplay I* at Hamburg.
April 1959: Commenced Cuxhaven-Montreal service.
December 1960: Refitted at Genoa; 680 all-first class passengers; year-round New York–Nassau cruise service.
April 1964: Sold to Canaveral International Corp, Bahamian flag, for $1.1 million for use as floating hotel at Freeport, Grand Bahama Island; renamed *Imperial Bahama Hotel;* given $1 million refit.
1965: Unsuccessful; later bankrupt and auctioned-off.
July 1965: Sold to Spanish shipbreakers for $700,000.
September 8, 1965: Arrived at Bilbao for scrapping.

Homeric

Service: Seasonal April–December: Cuxhaven (Hamburg)–Le Havre–Southampton–Quebec City–Montreal. Winter cruising from New York to the Caribbean.
Particulars: 24,907 gross tons; 638 × 79 feet.
Builders: Bethlehem Steel Co., Quincy, Massachusetts, 1931.
Machinery: Steam turbines; twin screw; service speed 20 knots.
Capacity: 147 first class and 1,096 tourist class.
July 18, 1931: Launched as *Mariposa* for Matson Navigation Co., U.S. flag.
February 2, 1932: Departed San Francisco on maiden voyage to Honolulu, South Pacific ports and Australia; 734 all-first class passengers.
1941–46: Troopship for American War Shipping Administration.

1946–53: Laid-up at Alameda, California; post war refit postponed.
1953: Sold to Home Lines, Panamanian flag; renamed *Homeric*.
1954: Major refit at Trieste; passenger accommodation increased from 734 to 1,243.
January 24, 1955: Departed from Venice on maiden crossing to New York; then Caribbean cruising.
May 3, 1955: Departed Quebec City on first crossing to Hamburg.
October 1963: Reassigned to fulltime cruising; 730 one-class passengers.
1964: New York–Nassau cruises.
1965: New York–Caribbean cruises.
September–October 1968: Refitted at Genoa.
July 1, 1973: Seriously damaged by galley and restaurant fire while off the New Jersey coast. Cruises canceled and withdrawn from service.
July 16, 1973: Arrived at Genoa; beyond economic repair.
January 29, 1974: Arrived at Kaohsiung, Taiwan, for scrapping.

The smart-looking *Italia* loading at Hamburg. (*ALF collection*)

The very popular *Homeric* arriving in at New York's Pier 84. (*ALF collection*)

24

Incres Line

Europa (1923)/*Nassau*

Service: 1950–51: Antwerp–Plymouth–New York; 1951–61: Annual voyages: Genoa–New York for overhauls, refits, etc.
Particulars: 15,044 gross tons; 573 × 72 × 30 feet.
Builders: Sir W. G. Armstrong-Whitworth & Co. Ltd., Newcastle, England, 1923.
Machinery: Steam turbines; twin screw; service speed 17 knots.
Capacity: 500 one-class passengers.

August 14, 1922: Launched as *Mongolia*, P&O Lines, British flag.
May 11, 1923: Departed London on maiden voyage to Sydney via Suez; 16,385 gross tons; 230 first class and 180 second class passengers.
1931: Passenger accommodation restyled as 800 third class; tonnage relisted as 16,956.
December 1938: Commenced charter to New Zealand Shipping Co.; renamed *Rimutaka*; London–Wellington service via Panama Canal.
1940–49: Troopship.
February 1950: Sold to Incres Compãnía de Navegación S/A (Incres Line), Panamanian flag; renamed *Europa*; rebuilt with accommodation for 500 one-class passengers.
July 5, 1951: Commenced New York–Antwerp service.
October 1951: Last sailing Antwerp to New York.
1952: Refitted for fulltime cruising; renamed *Nassau;* 617 one-class passengers; New York–Nassau cruises year-round.
June 1953: Coronation cruise: New York–London.
1954: Transferred to Liberian flag.
October 1961: Sold to Naviera Turistica Mexicana (Natumex Line), Mexican flag; renamed *Acapulco*; first liner under the Mexican flag. Refitted at Glasgow; lengthened to 575 feet; tonnage relisted as 15,182.
December 1961: Maiden cruise from New York to Acapulco via Panama postponed; ship detained by U.S. Coast Guard.
January 1961: Commenced Los Angeles–Mexico cruising; unsuccessful.
1962: Used as floating hotel at Seattle for World's Fair.
May 1963: Laid-up at Manzanillo, Mexico.
October 18, 1964: Departed Manzanillo in tow of Japanese tug *Benten Maru* for Osaka.
December 15, 1964: Arrived at Osaka; later scrapped.

Victoria

Service: Various annual transatlantic crossing: New York–Genoa, New York–Southampton–Amsterdam, etc. Year-round cruising from New York.
Particulars: 14,917 gross tons; 573 × 72 × 28 feet.
Builders: Harland & Wolff Ltd., Belfast, Northern Ireland, 1936.
Machinery: Fiat type diesels; twin screw; service speed 18 knots.
Capacity: 600 one-class passengers.
January 25, 1936: Launched as *Dunnottar Castle*, Union-Castle Line, British flag.
July 1936: Maiden voyage from Southampton Cape Town and Durban; then on London-around Africa service; 15,007 gross tons; 258 first class and 250 tourist class passengers.
October 1939: Became armed merchant cruiser.
1942: Became troopship.
1948: Decommissioned from war service. Major refit; 15,054 gross tons; accommodation restyled for 105 first class and 253 tourist class.
February 1949: Resumed London–around Africa service.
1958: Withdrawn and laid-up; later sold to Incres Steamship Co., Liberian flag; renamed *Victoria*. Towed to Schiedam, Holland and totally rebuilt; given new Fiat diesels replacing original B&W diesels; accommodation for 600 one-class passengers.
January 1960: Maiden voyage Le Havre to New York; then Caribbean cruising.
1964: Ownership transferred to Victoria Steamship Co., Liberian flag; continued under Incres Line operation.
August 1975: Bankruptcy of Incres Line; ship laid-up at Brooklyn.

November 1975: Sold to Chandris Group, Greek flag.
June 1976: Began Mediterranean and Black Sea cruising.
1977: Transferred to Phaidon Navigation S/A (Chandris Group), Panamanian flag; renamed *The Victoria*; Mediterranean and Caribbean cruising.
May 1980: Refit with forty-six cabins added.
May 1981: Sold to Victoria Maritime Corp (Chandris Group), Liberian flag; continued cruising.
1984: Resold to Phaidon Navigation S/A (Chandris Group), Panamanian flag. Tonnage relisted as 14,411.
1989: Tonnage relisted as 11,541.
1993: Sold to Louis Cruise Lines, Cypriot flag; renamed *Princesa Victoria*; capacity altered to 831 passengers.
1998: Used as floating hotel for Expo 98 at Lisbon.
1999: Laid-up in Perama Bay. Later used as hotel-ship for the G8 summit in Genoa in 2001.
2002: Laid-up.
2004: Scrapped by Kumar Steel Breakers Yard in Alang, India.

Above: The *Nassau* was the former P&O *Mongolia*. (*Mick Lindsay collection*)

Right: As *The Victoria*, the 1936-built ship departs from Lisbon. (*Luis Miguel Correia*)

Below: At the end of her days, the *Princesa Victoria* is laid-up in Perama Bay in Greece. The *Apollo* (ex-*Empress of Canada*) is on the far left. (*Philippe Brebant collection*)

25

International Catholic Travel Committee

Roma (1914)

Service: Charter crossings in 1950: Cherbourg–New York.
Particulars: 6,530 gross tons; 410 × 54 feet.
Builders: Newport News Shipbuilding & Dry Dock Co., Newport News, Virginia, 1914.
Machinery: Steam triple expansion engines; single screw; service speed 14 knots.
Capacity: 950 one-class passengers.

August 22, 1914: Launched as freighter *Medina* for Mallory Steamship Co., U.S. flag; American West Coast service.
1934: Transferred to AGWI Lines, also U.S. flag; continued in coastal services.
1941–45: Wartime service as a transport including transatlantic voyages.
1948: Sold to Compañía San Miguel S/A, Panamanian flag; rebuilt at La Spezia as passenger ship with 950 berths; renamed *Roma.*
1950: Atlantic crossings plus Europe–Australia migrant voyages.
1952: Mechanically exhausted, but sold to Costa Line, Italian flag; renamed *Franca C*; re-engined with Fiat diesels; 925 passengers in three classes. Genoa–East Coast of South America service.
1959: Rebuilt as cruise ship for 350 all-first class passengers. Mediterranean cruises from Genoa in summer; Caribbean cruises from Port Everglades in winter.
1970: Another extensive refit; another set of Fiat diesels installed.
1977: Sold to Operation Mobilisation, Maltese flag; used as internationally-roving book display and library; worldwide service; further refits and extensions; renamed *Doulos.*
2009: Operating certificate revoked at the age of ninety-five; sold to Singapore buyers; renamed *Doulos Phos*; intention to use the ship as hotel and museum; project never materialized.

The *Roma* but seen as Costa's *Franca C.* (*Gillespie-Faber collection*)

Rusted and laid-up, the *Liguria* reaches the end of her days. (*Cronican-Arroyo collection*)

2014: Reached 100th year.
2015: Sold to Indonesian buyers; towed to Batan Island; refitted as a luxury hotel; then towed to Bintan Island.
October 2015: Refitted with strengthened hull and superstructure.
2016: Ship hoisted up a slope; repositioned to overlook the harbor of Bintan Island.

Liguria

Service: Charter crossings in 1950: New York–Cherbourg or Dublin.
Particulars: 7,474 gross tons; 442 × 55 feet.
Builders: Reiherstieg & Co., Hamburg, Germany, 1917.
Machinery: Quadruple expansion engines; twin screw; service speed 14 knots.
Capacity: 929 one-class passengers.

June 6, 1914: Launched as *Hilda Woermann* for Woermann Line, German flag; then completion delayed by World War I.
1917: Renamed *Wahehe.*
November 1918: Claimed by the British as prize of war.
1919–20: U.K.–Australia service as *Wahehe*, British flag, managed by Shaw Savill Line.
November 1920: Purchased by Burns Philp Line, Australian flag; renamed *Marella*; refitted at Sydney.
1921–41: Sydney-Singapore service; 165 first-class and seventy-five second-class passengers.
1941–46: Used as troopship.
1946–48: Resumed Sydney–Singapore service.
November 1948: Final voyage then sold to Compañía Navegación Baru, Panamanian flag; renamed *Captain Marcos*; refitted in Italy for 929 passengers.
October 1949: One voyage as *Captain Marcos* then renamed *Liguria.*
June 1950: Began series of transatlantic crossings.
January 1951: Mechanical breakdown off Australia; eight months of repairs; renamed *Corsica* for same owners.
1952: Migrant voyages to Australia but later arrested for debt.
August 1952: Laid-up at Casablanca.
October 1954: Sold to Belgian shipbreakers.
November 14, 1954: Arrived at Ghent for demolition.

26

Italian Line

Conte Biancamano

Service: Genoa–Cannes–Naples–Palermo–Gibraltar–Halifax (westbound only)–New York; call at Boston (eastbound). Otherwise Genoa––East Coast of South America service.
Particulars: 23,842 gross tons; 665 × 76 × 26 feet.
Builders: William Beardmore & Co., Glasgow, Scotland, 1925.
Machinery: Steam turbines; geared to twin screw; service speed 18 knots.
Capacity: 215 first class passengers, 333 cabin class, and 1,030 tourist class.

April 23, 1925: Launched as *Conte Biancamano* for Lloyd Sabaudo, Italian flag.
November 1925: Completed; Genoa–Naples–New York service.
1932: Transferred to Italian Line; Genoa–East Coast of South America service.
1937: Transferred to Lloyd Triestino; Genoa–Far East service.
1939: Transferred to Italian Liner; Genoas–East Coast of South America service.
December 1941: Seized by U.S. Government at Cristobal; refitted for U.S. Navy as troopship *Hermitage*.
August 1946: Decommissioned by U.S. Navy; laid-up.
August 1947: Returned to Italian Line; renamed *Conte Biancamano*; major refit and restoration.
November 10, 1949: Departed Genoa on post-war maiden voyage to East Coast of South America.
1950–59: Summer season service to New York.
April 1960: Laid-up at Naples.
August 16, 1960: Arrived at La Spezia for scrapping.

Conte Grande

Service: Normally Genoa–East Coast of South America, but substitute sailing in 1956: Genoa–Naples–Palermo–Gibraltar–New York.
Particulars: 23,562 gross tons; 667 × 78 × 27 feet.
Builders: Stabilimento Tecnico, Trieste, Italy, 1928.
Machinery: Steam turbines; geared to twin screw; service speed 18 knots.
Capacity: 261 first class, 338 cabin class, and 780 passengers.

June 29, 1927: Launched as *Conte Grande* for Lloyd Sabaudo, Italian flag.
April 1928: Entered Genoa–Naples–New York service.
1932: Transferred to Italian Line.
1933: Transferred to Genoa–East Coast of South America service.
1940: Laid-up at Santos owing to war in Europe.
August 22, 1941: Transferred to U.S. Navy at Santos; refitted as a troopship; renamed *Monticello*.
March 22, 1946: Decommissioned by U.S. Navy; laid-up.
July 23, 1947: Returned to Italian Line; renamed *Conte Grande*; major refit and restoration.
July 14, 1949: Commenced Genoa-East Coast of South America service.
September 1956: Roundtrip voyage to New York as substitute for sunken *Andrea Doria*.
December 1960: Charter voyage Italy–Australia for Lloyd Triestino; then laid-up.
September 7, 1961: Arrived at La Spezia for scrapping.

Saturnia

Service: 1947–55: Genoa–Naples–Gibraltar–New York; 1955–65: Trieste–Venice–Patras–Messina or Palermo–Naples–Gibraltar–Halifax (westbound only)–New York. Occasional calls at Boston (eastbound only), Lisbon, Barcelona, and Dubrovnik.
Particulars: 24,346 gross tons; 630 × 80 × 29 feet.
Builders: Cantieri Navali Triestino, Monfalcone, Italy, 1927.

Handsomely rebuilt after the War, the *Conte Biancamano* looks quite contemporary. (*Gillespie-Faber collection*)

The *Conte Grande* at berth at Genoa as the *Conte Biancamano* departs in the upper left. (*Author's collection*)

Machinery: Sulzer diesels; geared to single screw; service speed 19 knots.
Capacity: 255 first class, 270 cabin class, and 954 tourist class passengers.

December 29, 1925: Launched for Cosulich Line, Italian flag.
September 1927: Completed as *Saturnia*; Trieste–Venice–East Coast of South America service.
February 1928: Transferred to Trieste–Venice–New York service.
1932: Transferred to Italian Line.
1935: Trooping to East Africa for Italian Government.
1935–36: Major refit; original B&W type diesels replaced with more powerful Sulzer diesels; service speed increased to 21 knots; tonnage relisted as 24,470.
June 1940: Laid-up at Trieste owing to war.
September 1943: Left Italy and later taken over by U.S. Government for trooping.
January–June 1945: Refitted and used as U.S. Navy hospital ship; renamed *Francis Y. Slanger*.
November 1945: Decommissioned as hospital ship.
February 1946: Resumed trooping services.
December 1, 1946: Returned to Italian Line; renamed *Saturnia*; later major refit and restoration.
August 29, 1947: Left Genoa on first post-war sailing for Italian Line.
November 1955: Transferred to Trieste–Venice–New York service.
April 11, 1965: Laid-up at Trieste.
October 7, 1965: Arrived under tow at La Spezia; sold to local scrappers for $1 million.
April 1966: Demolition began.

Vulcania

Service: Italy–New York (same as *Saturnia*).
Particulars: 24,496 gross tons; 631 × 80 × 29 feet.
Builders: Cantieri Navali Triestino, Monfalcone, Italy, 1928.
Machinery: Fiat type diesels; geared to twin screw; service speed 19 knots.
Capacity: 232 first class, 262 cabin class, and 958 tourist class passengers.
1926: Laid down for Cosulich Line; intended to be named *Urania*.

December 16, 1926: Launched as *Vulcania*.
December 19, 1928: Departed Trieste on maiden voyage to New York; 279 first class, 257 second class, 310 third class and 1,350 fourth class.
1932: Transferred to Italian Line.
1935: Trooping to East Africa for Italian Government.
May–December 1935: Major refit: Original B&W type diesels replaced by more powerful Fiat diesels.
June 1940: Withdrawn from transatlantic service owing to war; later some trooping for Italian Government.
1941: Laid-up at Trieste.
September 1943: Made a dash away from Italy.
October 1943: Became U.S. Army transport.
1946: Made some austerity crossings to Le Havre and Southampton for United States Lines.
December 14, 1946: Decommissioned by U.S. Government; returned to Italian Line; later major refit and restoration.
September 1947: Resumed Italian Line sailings to New York.
October 1955: Transferred to Trieste–Venice–New York service.
May 1965: Laid-up at Trieste; later sold to Grimaldi-Siosa Lines, also Italian flag; renamed *Caribia*; refitted for 337 first class, 368 cabin class, and 732 tourist class passengers.
January 12, 1966: First sailing as *Caribia* from Venice.
February 28, 1966: First sailing from Southampton to the West Indies.

The *Saturnia* loads passengers at Naples. (*ALF collection*)

September 29, 1972: Laid-up at La Spezia.
January 1973: Reportedly sold to Italian shipbreakers, but then resold to Spanish breakers instead.
September 18, 1973: Arrived at Barcelona.
February 1974: Resold to Taiwanese scrappers.
March 15, 1974: Left Barcelona under tow for Kaohsiung.
July 1974: Arrived Kaohsiung.
July 20, 1974: Sank in Kaohsiung harbor owing to leakages; later raised and scrapped.

Giulio Cesare

Service: 1956–59: Naples–Genoa–Cannes–Gibraltar–New York; otherwise, Genoa–East Coast of South America.
Particulars: 27,078 gross tons; 681 × 87 × 28 feet.
Builders: Cantieri Riuniti dell'Adriatico, Monfalcone, Italy, 1951.
Machinery: Fiat type diesels; geared to twin; service speed 21 knots.
Capacity: 181 first class, 288 cabin class, and 714 tourist class.

May 18, 1950: Launched; fitted with diesels made in 1939.
October 1951: Maiden voyage: Genoa-South America.
June 29, 1956: Departed Genoa on first seasonal voyage to New York.
1960: Permanently returned to Genoa–South America service.
December 1964: Became two-class ship: 181 first class and 1,000 tourist class.
December 1972: Serious rudder trouble during Genoa–Buenos Aires voyage.
January 14, 1973: Laid-up at Naples.
May 11, 1973: Arrived under tow at La Spezia for scrapping.

Augustus

Service: 1957–60: Italy–New York (same as *Giulio Cesare*); otherwise, Italy–East Coast of South America.
Particulars: 27,090 gross tons; 680 × 87 × 28 feet.
Builders: Cantieri Riuniti dell'Adriatico, Trieste, Italy, 1952.
Machinery: Fiat type diesels; geared to twin screw; service speed 21 knots.
Capacity: 180 first class, 280 cabin class, and 714 tourist class.

November 19, 1950: Launched.
February 1952: Maiden voyage: Genoa–Buenos Aires.
February 7, 1957: Departed Genoa on first voyage to New York.
1960: Permanently assigned to Genoa–South America run.

Motor Ship Style: The *Vulcania* at Genoa. (*ALF collection*)

Seen at Malta, the former *Vulcania* is seen as the *Caribia*. (*Michael Cassar collection*)

Seen from the stern of the *Andrea Doria*, the *Vulcania* departs. (*ALF collection*)

The *Giulio Cesare* arriving in Boston in 1957. (*Anton Logvinenko*)

Underway: The westbound *Augustus* as seen from the eastbound *Giulio Cesare*. (*ALF collection*)

December 1964: Became two-class ship: 180 first class and 1,000 tourist class.
January 16, 1976: Laid-up at Naples; later sold to Great Shipping & Investment Ltd., Seychelles flag; renamed *Great Sea*; sailed to Hong Kong for refit.
July 1977: Transferred to Great Sea Shipping Co., Panamanian flag; to Keelung for further refitting.
October 1977: Moved to Hong Kong; laid-up.
July 1978: Sailed Hong Kong–Kaohsiung–Keelung–Hong Kong; resumed lay-up.
1980: Sold to Ocean King Navigation Co., Philippines flag; renamed *Ocean King*.
January 1982: Moved to Manila and laid-up.
1983: Renamed *Philippines*; used as accommodation ship at Manila.
1985: Renamed *President*.
1987: Moved from Manila to Hong Kong and then to Keelung.
November 1987: Sold to Philtrust Finance Ltd., Hong Kong; renamed *Asian Princess*.
1990: Changed to Philippines registry; returned to Manila. Used partially as a maritime training school.
October 1999: Renamed *Philippines* and in use as hotel and convention center.
2000: Rumored to be bought by Italian investors and returned to Genoa for use as a maritime museum; never materialized.
October 11, 2011: Arrived at Alang under tow for scrapping.

Andrea Doria

Service: Genoa–Cannes–Naples–Gibraltar–New York; some winter cruising from New York to the Caribbean.
Particulars: 29,083 gross tons; 700 × 90 × 30 feet.
Builders: Ansaldo Shipyard, Genoa, Italy, 1952.
Machinery: Steam turbines; geared to twin screw; service speed 23 knots.
Capacity: 218 first class, 320 cabin class, and 703 tourist.

June 16, 1951: Launched.
January 14, 1953: Left Genoa on maiden voyage to New York.
July 26, 1956: Sank after collision with Swedish-American liner *Stockholm* (qv) off Nantucket; fifty-two casualties.

Cristoforo Colombo

Service: 1954–65: Genoa–Cannes–Naples–Gibraltar–New York; 1965–73: Trieste–Venice–Piraeus–Messina–Palermo–Naples–Halifax (westbound only)–New York. Boston occasionally on eastbound crossings; also occasionally include Lisbon and Barcelona.
Particulars: 29,181 gross tons; 700 × 90 × 30 feet.
Builders: Ansaldo Shipyard, Genoa, Italy, 1954.
Machinery: Steam turbines; geared to single screw; service speed 23 knots.
Capacity: 301 first class, 242 cabin class, and 703 tourist class.

January 19, 1952: Laid down.
May 10, 1953: Launched.
July 15, 1954: Left Genoa on maiden voyage to New York.
January 1963: Major refit: Tonnage relisted as 29,429; accommodation restyled as 208 first class, 304 cabin class, and 558 tourist class.
June 1965: Transferred to Trieste–Venice–New York service.
August 1966: Repainted with white hull.
February 1973: Transferred to Genoa–East Coast of South America service.
April 1977: Sold to Venezuelan Government for £3.4 million; for use as workers' accommodation ship.
May 15, 1977: Left Genoa for Matanzas, Venezuela.

The *Philippines* (the former *Augustus*) seen at Manila in her final years. (*ALF collection*)

Departing from Naples: The outbound *Andrea Doria*. (*ALF collection*)

The *Cristoforo Colombo* at Lisbon. (*ALF collection*)

July 1977: Began use as hotel ship at Puerto Ordaz, Venezuela.
1978: Owners identified as CVG Siderurgica Del Orinoco S/A.
1980: Offered for sale; later sold to Taiwanese scrappers.
March 12, 1981: Broke loose in the mouth of the Orinoco River while being towed to Taiwan; later reconnected.
June 30, 1981: Arrived Kaohsiung under tow; offered for resale.
May 1982: Moved to Hong Kong; still offered for sale.
July 23, 1983: Towed to Kaohsiung then scrapped.

Leonardo da Vinci

Service: Genoa–Cannes–Naples–Gibraltar–New York; occasional calls at other Mediterranean ports as well as occasional calls at Halifax (westbound) and Boston (eastbound); also considerable cruising.
Particulars: 33,340 gross tons; 761 × 92 × 30 feet.
Builders: Ansaldo Shipyard, Genoa, Italy, 1960.
Machinery: Steam turbines; geared to twin screw; service speed 23 knots.
Capacity: 413 first class, 342 cabin class, and 571 tourist class.
Notes: Built so as to be eventually converted to nuclear power; never materialized.

June 23, 1957: Laid down.
December 7, 1958: Launched.
June 30, 1960: Departed Genoa on maiden crossing to New York.
February 1966: Repainted with white hull.
February 27, 1970: Departed New York on special forty-one-day cruise to Hawaiian Islands via Panama.
June 1976: Made final Italian Line transatlantic sailing
July 1977: Transferred to Italian Line Cruises International; managed by Costa Line; 900 one-class passengers; Miami–Nassau cruises.
1978: Use as cruise ship: unsuccessful.
September 23, 1978: Laid-up at La Spezia; offered for sale; later rumored to become a floating entertainment center and casino moored on the River Thames.
June 4, 1979: Suffered damage from burning freighter *Da Recco* laid-up alongside.
January 1980: Rumored to be sold to Trident Maritime Corp, Panamanian flag, for Caribbean cruising from New York and Port Everglades; never materialized.
July 3, 1980: Caught fire; towed to outer harbor; burnt out; later capsized in shallow water.
March 31, 1981: Refloated.
May 6, 1982: Demolition began by Cantieri Navali Lotti at La Spezia.

Michelangelo

Service: Naples–Genoa–Cannes–Gibraltar–New York; occasional calls at Barcelona, Lisbon, Casablanca, and Madeira.
Particulars: 45,911 gross tons; 902 × 102 × 34 feet.
Builders: Ansaldo Shipyard, Genoa, Italy, 1965.
Machinery: Steam turbines; geared to twin screw; service speed 26½ knots.

Homeport: The beautiful *Leonardo da Vinci* at Genoa. (*ALF collection*)

Maiden Arrival: The *Michelangelo* is berthed at Pier 90, New York in this May 1965 photo. (*Moran Towing & Transportation Co.*)

Capacity: 535 first class, 550 cabin class, and 690 tourist class; 1,200 one-class passengers for cruising.

September 16, 1962: Launched; initially intended to have a black hull.
May 12, 1965: Left Genoa on maiden voyage to New York.
December 31, 1965: First overhaul began; propellers changed; new trial speed of 31.59 knots.
April 12, 1966: Struck by 50-foot waves in North Atlantic storm; two killed; extensive damage.
June 1975: Withdrawn and laid-up at La Spezia.
November 1975: Reportedly sold to I. G. Tornado, Liechtenstein, for use as floating cancer research-treatment center; sale never materialized. Also considered by Home Lines, Norwegian Caribbean Lines and as moored housing at Santos, Brazil; none materialized.
February 1977: Sold Iranian Navy for $4 million.
July 8, 1977: Departed Genoa for Bandar Abbas via Suez.
July 21, 1977: Arrived at Bandar Abbas for use as Iranian naval accommodation ship: 500 officers and 1,300 cadet-mariners.
1978: Considered to be restored by Iranian interests for use as cruise ship; to be renamed *Reza Shah the Great*; never materialized.
February 1979: Following Islamic Revolution in Iran, ship fell into declining condition.
September 1986: Reportedly sold to Taiwanese breakers; never materialized.
July 1991: Towed from Bandar Abbas to Gadani Beach, Pakistan to be scrapped.

Raffaello

Service: Naples–Genoa–Cannes–Gibraltar–New York; occasional calls at Barcelona, Lisbon, Casablanca, and Madeira.
Particulars: 45,933 gross tons; 902 × 102 × 34 feet.
Builders: Cantieri Riuniti dell'Adriatico, Trieste, Italy, 1965.
Machinery: Steam turbines; geared to twin screw; service speed 26½ knots.
Capacity: 535 first class, 550 cabin class, and 690 tourist class; 1,200 one-class passengers for cruising.

March 24, 1962: Launched; initially intended to have a black hull.
July 25, 1965: Left Genoa on maiden voyage to New York.
October 31, 1965: Engine room fire.
May 18, 1970: Collision in Algeciras Bay with tanker *Cuyahoga*.
February 1971: Rumored to be transferred to Genoa–East Coast of South America service; never materialized.
May 1975: Withdrawn and laid-up at La Spezia.
November 1975: Reportedly sold to I. G. Tornado, Liechtenstein, for use as floating cancer research-treatment center; sale never materialized. Also considered by Home Lines, Norwegian Caribbean Lines and as moored housing at Santos, Brazil; none materialized.
February 1977: Sold Iranian Navy for $4 million.
August 1977: Arrived at Bushehr for use as Iranian naval accommodation ship: 500 officers and 1,300 cadet-mariners.
1978: Considered to be restored by Iranian interests for use as cruise ship; to be renamed *Cyrus the Great*; never materialized.
February 1979: Following Islamic Revolution in Iran, ship fell into declining condition.
February 1983: Bombed and sunk at Bushehr during Iran–Iraq War; wreckage further damaged when freighter *Iran Salam* sank above *Raffaello*.
2006: Talk of salvage; never materialized.
2015: Further talk of salvage; never materialized.

Dominated by her winged funnels, the *Raffaello* departs from Naples. (*Mick Lindsay collection)*

Lonely Isolation: The *Michelangelo* and *Raffaello* are "nested" together at La Spezia in this 1976 scene. (*Author's collection*)

27

Jugolinija

Hrvatska

Service: Variable: Rijeka–Trieste–Naples–Casablanca–New York (and other U.S. East Coast ports: Baltimore, Philadelphia, Norfolk, etc.)
Particulars: 7,904 gross tons; 455 × 62 × 28 feet.
Builders: Permanent Shipyard No. 2, Richmond, California, 1945.
Machinery: Steam turbines; single screw; service speed 17 knots.
Capacity: Sixty to seventy-five one-class passengers.

March 1945: Completed as *St Lawrence Victory* for U.S. War Shipping Administration, U.S. flag; Victory Class freighter-transport.
March 25, 1947: Struck a mine 8 miles off Dubrovnik; abandoned in sinking condition; later towed by trawlers to Korčula and then to Split. U.S. authorities abandoned her ship and then claimed by Yugoslavian Government; renamed *Zagreb*. Later repaired and refitted with sixty passenger berths.
September 20, 1949: Left Rijeka on maiden voyage to New York, but as *Hrvatska*.
1967: Sold to Adab S/A of Geneva, flag of African kingdom of Burundi; then resold to Compañía Naviera Adriatica Ltd., Costa Rican flag.
1968: Sold again to Société Des Avances Commerciales S/A, Somali Republic flag; renamed *Armelle;* general tramp service.
September 3, 1972: Arrived at Bilbao, Spain, for scrapping.

Srbija

Service: Variable: Rijeka–New York (same ports as *Hrvatska)*
Particulars: 6,634 gross tons; 475 × 60 × 25 feet.
Builders: A. Vuyk & Zonen, IJssel, Holland, 1949.
Machinery: Sulzer diesels; single screw; service speed 15 knots.
Capacity: Forty-four in first and tourist class; later all one-class.
1944: Launched as freighter *Crostafels*, Hansa Line, German flag; remained incomplete owing to the War.
1949: Transferred to Yugoslavia and then to Jugolinija; completed as *Drvar* and then renamed *Srbija.*

A converted Victory ship, Jugolinija's *Hrvatska* could carry up to seventy-five passengers. (*Author's collection*)

October 17, 1949: Departure from Rijeka on maiden voyage to New York.
1970: Reduced to freighter; worldwide tramp service.
1980: Operating on Yugoslavia–Suez–Persian Gulf service.
1983: Scrapped in China.

Visevica

Service: Variously Rijeka–Naples–Genoa–New York and other U.S. East Coast ports (Philadelphia, Baltimore, Norfolk, etc.).
Particulars: 6,750 gross tons; 492 × 65 feet.
Builders: 3 Maj Shipyard, Rijeka, Yugoslavia, 1964.
Machinery: Sulzer diesels; single screw; service speed 18 knots.
Capacity: Twenty first class and thirty tourist class.

February 7, 1966: Heavy damage following collision with American Pioneer Lines' freighter *Pioneer Myth* off New Jersey coast; later repaired.
1980: Sold to Rashid Shipping Co., Egyptian flag; renamed *Abu Hosna*; short-lived passenger-cargo service to U.S. East Coast ports but unsuccessful.
1982: Laid-up; later sold to Samatour Shipping Co., also Egyptian flag; renamed *Salem S*; used in general tramping service.
1993: Sold to Indian scrappers; renamed *Zoe S* for final voyage to Alang.

Klek

Service: Variously Rijeka–Naples–Genoa–New York and other U.S. East Coast ports (Philadelphia, Baltimore, Norfolk, etc.).
Particulars: 6,750 gross tons; 492 × 65 feet.
Builders: 3 Maj Shipyard, Rijeka, Yugoslavia, 1965.
Machinery: Sulzer diesels; single screw; service speed 18 knots.
Capacity: Twenty first class and thirty tourist class.
1980: Sold to Rashid Shipping Co., Egyptian flag; renamed *Abu Alia*; short-lived passenger-cargo service to U.S. East Coast ports but unsuccessful.
1982: Laid-up; later sold to Samatour Shipping Co., also Egyptian flag; renamed *Salem A*; used in general tramping service.
1991: Scrapped.

Tuhobic

Service: Variously Rijeka–Naples–Genoa–New York and other U.S. East Coast ports (Philadelphia, Baltimore, Norfolk, etc.).
Particulars: 6,750 gross tons; 492 × 65 feet.
Builders: 3 Maj Shipyard, Rijeka, Yugoslavia, 1964.
Machinery: Sulzer diesels; single screw; service speed 18 knots.
Capacity: Twenty first class and thirty tourist class.

1980: Sold to Rashid Shipping Co., Egyptian flag; renamed *Abu Rashid*; short-lived passenger-cargo service to U.S. East Coast ports but unsuccessful.
1982: Laid-up; later sold to Samatour Shipping Co., also Egyptian flag; used in general tramping service.
1991: Scrapped.

Zvir

Service: Variously Rijeka–Naples–Genoa–New York and other U.S. East Coast ports (Philadelphia, Baltimore, Norfolk, etc.).
Particulars: 6,750 gross tons; 492 × 65 feet.
Builders: 3 Maj Shipyard, Rijeka, Yugoslavia, 1964.
Machinery: Sulzer diesels; single screw; service speed 18 knots.
Capacity: Twenty first class and thirty tourist class.

1980: Sold to Rashid Shipping Co., Egyptian flag; renamed *Abu Yossuf I*; short-lived passenger-cargo service to U.S. East Coast ports but unsuccessful.
1982: Laid-up; later sold to Samatour Shipping Co., also Egyptian flag; used in general tramping service.
1990: Scrapped.

28

Khedivial Mail Line

Khedive Ismail/Cleopatra

Service: Ports varied: Alexandria–Beirut–Naples–Leghorn–Genoa–Marseilles–New York–U.S. East Coast ports (Philadelphia, Baltimore, Norfolk, etc.).
Particulars: 8,193 gross tons; 455 × 62 × 28 feet.
Builders: Oregon Shipbuilding Corp, Portland, Oregon, 1944.
Machinery: Steam turbines; single screw; service speed 15 knots.
Capacity: 100 all-first class passengers.
Notes: First Victory Ship built in America.

November 13, 1943: Keel laid.
January 12, 1944: Launched as *United Victory* for War Shipping Administration, U.S. flag; Victory Class freighter-transport.
February 28, 1944: Completed; constructed in just over three months.
1946: Declared surplus: Sold to Renfrew Navigation Co. (Furness Withy & Co.), British flag; freighter service.
1947: Renamed *Khedive Ismail.*
1948: Sold to Khedivial Mail Line, Egyptian flag; rebuilt at Alexandria with 100 passenger berths.
1954: Began extended service to Karachi and Bombay via Suez.
1956: Renamed *Cleopatra.*
1960: Transferred to United Arab Co; route changed to Eastern Canada, Northern Europe, etc. according to inducement (qv).

Mohammed Ali El Kebir

Service: Alexandria–New York (ports see *Khedive Ismail*).
Particulars: 8,199 gross tons; 455 × 62 × 28 feet.
Builders: California Shipbuilding Corp., Los Angeles, California, 1944.
Machinery: Steam turbines; single screw; service speed 15 knots.
Capacity: 100 all-first class passengers.

June 1944: Commissioned as *Atchison Victory* for War Shipping Administration, U.S. flag; Victory Class freighter-transport.
1946: Declared surplus: Sold to Renfrew Navigation Co. (Furness Withy & Co.), British flag; freighter service.
1947: Renamed *Mohammed Ali El Kebir*
1948: Sold to Khedivial Mail Line, Egyptian flag; rebuilt at Alexandria with 100 passenger berths.
1954: Began extended service to Karachi and Bombay via Suez.
1960: Transferred to United Arab Co.; renamed *Salah El Din;* route changed to Eastern Canada, Northern Europe, etc. according to inducement (qv).

Gumhuryat Misr

Service: 1954–55: Alexandria–Beirut–Naples–Leghorn–Genoa–Marseilles–Charleston–Philadelphia–New London (Connecticut)–New York; return via various Mediterranean ports to Alexandria.
Particulars: 7,830 gross tons; 437 × 59 × 24 feet.
Builders: Cammell Laird & Co., Birkenhead, England, 1928.
Machinery: Steam turbines; twin screw; service speed 14 knots.
Capacity: 118 first class and 115 tourist, plus dormitory quarters for pilgrims when needed.

1928–39: Sailed in Halifax–Boston–Bermuda–West Indies–British Guiana service as *Lady Nelson* for Canadian National Steamships Ltd., Canadian flag.
September 1939: requisitioned for war service.

1942: Damaged by torpedo at St. Lucia; later repaired and refitted as Canadian hospital ship.
1945–46: Repatriation service.
1947–52: Resumed Caribbean service.
October 1952: Sold to Khedivial Mail Line, Egyptian flag; renamed *Gumhuryat Misr*; refitted at Alexandria; 120 first-class and 130 tourist-class passengers.
March 5, 1954: Departed from Alexandria on first voyage to New York and other U.S. East Coast ports.
1955: Final transatlantic voyage: Alexandria–Mediterranean ports–New Orleans–New York–Mediterranean ports–Alexandria. Thereafter confined to inter-Mediterranean services and periodic voyages carrying pilgrims to Jeddah.
1960: Renamed *Al Wadi.*
1962: Transferred to United Arab Maritime Co., Egyptian flag.
1968: Scrapped.

Egypt's *Mohammed Ali El Kebir* berthed at New Orleans. (*Gillespie-Faber collection*)

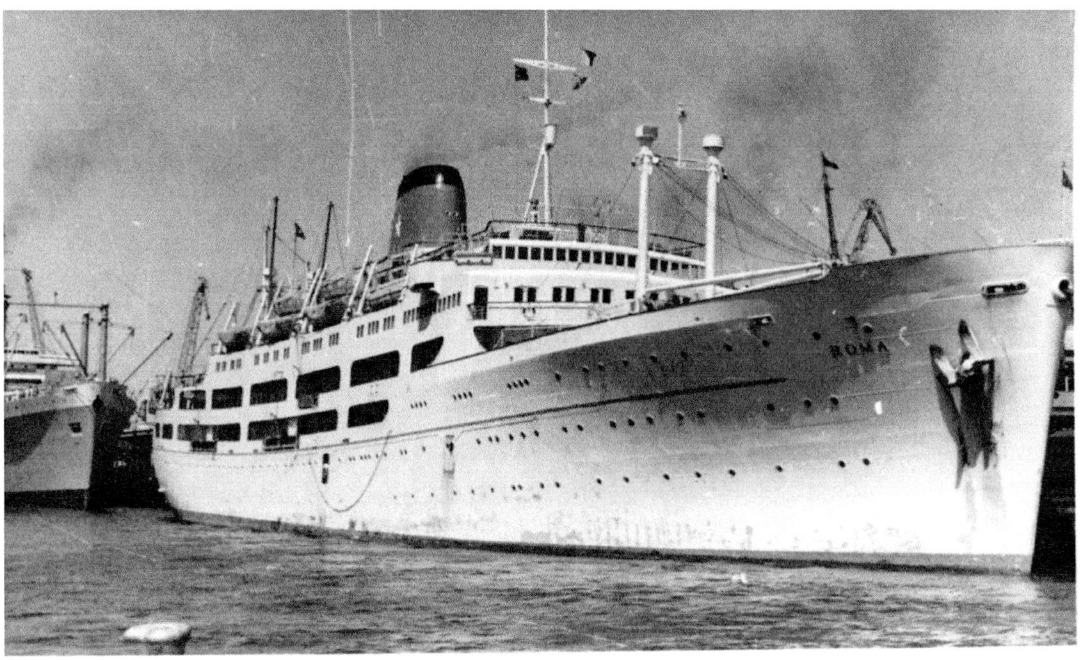

29

Lauro Line

Sydney

Service: 1953: Liverpool–Quebec City sailings.
Particulars: 14,708 gross tons; 492 × 69 × 27 feet.
Builders: Western Pipe & Steel Co., San Francisco, California, 1943.
Machinery: Steam turbines; single screw; service speed 17 knots.
Capacity: Ninety-four first class and 708 tourist class.
Notes: Auxiliary aircraft carrier converted into passenger ship.

1941–42: Constructed as standard C-3 Class freighter but then redesigned as auxiliary aircraft carrier for U.S. Navy; named *USS Croatan*.
April 9, 1942: Launched; then transferred to Royal Navy, British flag; renamed *HMS Fencer*.
February 1943: Entered service.
1943–46: War duties.
December 1946: Returned to U.S. Navy.
1946–50: Laid-up.
1950: Sold to Flotta Lauro (Lauro Line), Italian flag; renamed *Sydney*; rebuilt at Genoa as a passenger ship.
September 1951: Entered Genoa–Australia service.
1953: Liverpool–Quebec City sailings.
1954–66: Genoa–Australia service.
December 1967: Renamed *Roma* for same owners; cruising only.
1969: Sold to Aretusa SpA, Italian flag; cruising only.
October 1970: Laid-up at La Spezia.
January 1971: Sold to Sovereign Cruises Ltd., Cypriot flag, for $1 million; renamed *Galaxy Queen*. Refitted for Mediterranean cruise service; 900 one-class passengers.
1973: Sold to George Kotsovilis, Greek flag; renamed *Lady Dina*. Later resold to Marimina Shipping Co. S/A, Italian flag; renamed *Caribia 2*.
February 1975: Sold to Italian shipbreakers at La Spezia for 760 million lire.
September 1, 1975: Demolition began.

Roma

Service: 1953–56: Naples–Genoa–Barcelona–Gibraltar–Halifax (westbound only–New York–Gibraltar–Genoa–Naples.
Particulars: 14,687 gross tons; 492 × 69 × 27 feet.
Builders: Seattle-Tacoma Shipbuilding Corp., Tacoma, Washington, 1943.
Machinery: Steam turbines; single screw; service speed 17 knots.
Capacity: Ninety-four first class and 708 tourist class.
Notes: Auxiliary aircraft carrier converted into passenger ship.

1941–42: Constructed as standard C-3 Class freighter but then redesigned as auxiliary aircraft carrier for U.S. Navy; named *USS Glacier.*
April 9, 1942: Launched.
July 31, 1943: Transferred to Royal Navy, British flag; renamed *HMS Fencer*.
1943–46: War duties.
December 1946: Returned to U.S. Navy.
1947–50: Laid-up.
1950: Sold to Flotta Lauro (Lauro Line), Italian flag; renamed *Roma*; rebuilt at Genoa as a passenger ship.
August 1951: Entered Genoa–Australia service.
May 1953: Commenced Mediterranean–New York service.
November 30, 1956: Left New York on final transatlantic crossing; resumed Genoa–Australia sailings fulltime.
1960: Major refit: Passenger accommodation increased to 119 first class and 994 tourist class; tonnage relisted as 14,976.
1966: Transferred to Genoa–West Indies service.
November 2, 1967: Arrived at Vado, Italy, for scrapping.

Previous page, below: The *Roma* berthed at Melbourne with the *Orcades* just behind. (*Lindsay Johnstone collection*)

30

National Hellenic American Line

Queen Frederica

Service: Piraeus–Naples–Palermo–Gibraltar–Halifax (westbound only)–New York–Boston (occasionally)–Gibraltar–Naples–Palermo–Piraeus. Winter cruising from New York to Bermuda, Bahamas, and Caribbean.
Particulars: 20,553 gross tons; 582 × 83 × 29 feet.
Builders: William Cramp & Sons Ship & Engine Building Co., Camden, New Jersey, 1927.
Machinery: Steam turbines; twin screw; service speed 21 knots.
Capacity: 132 first class, 116 cabin class, and 931 tourist class; often merged into one-class. 650 one-class for cruising from New York.

1927–37: Sailed as *Malolo*, Matson Navigation Co., U.S. flag.
1937–48: Renamed *Matsonia*, Matson Navigation Co., U.S. flag.
1948: Sold to Home Lines, Panamanian flag; renamed *Atlantic* (qv).
December 1954: Transferred to National Hellenic American Line, Greek flag; renamed *Queen Frederica* (qv).
November 1965: Sold to Chandris Group (Themistocles Navigation S/A), Greek flag (qv).

The *Queen Frederica* had a long and largely successful career of some fifty years. (*Gillespie-Faber collection*)

31

Netherlands Government

Zuiderkruis

Service: Summer season sailings between Rotterdam and New York or Quebec City; occasionally via Le Havre and Southampton. At other times to Australia, South Africa, Indonesia, etc.
Particulars: 9,178 gross tons; 455 × 62 × 28 feet.
Builders: Oregon Shipbuilding Corp., Portland, Oregon, 1944.
Machinery: Steam turbines; single screw; service speed 16 knots.
Capacity: 900 one-class passengers.
Notes: Former freighter rebuilt as a passenger ship.

May 1944: Delivered as *Cranston Victory* to War Shipping Administration, U.S. flag; Victory class freighter.
1947: Sold to Dutch Government, Dutch flag for trooping; managed by Royal Rotterdam Lloyd; renamed *Zuiderkruis.*
1951: Rebuilt as a migrant/low fare passenger ship by Netherlands Dock Co., Amsterdam; managed by Nederland Line.
July 1951: Left Rotterdam on maiden voyage to Quebec City.
1960: Transferred to Trans-Ocean Steamship Co., Dutch flag; continued in transatlantic service.
January 1963: Transferred to Dutch Navy for use as an accommodation and stores ship at Den Helder; designated A-853.
November 27, 1969: Arrived at Bilbao, Spain, for scrapping.

Groote Beer

Service: Summer season sailings between Rotterdam and New York or Quebec City; occasionally via Le Havre and Southampton. At other times to Australia, South Africa, Indonesia, etc.
Particulars: 9,190 gross tons; 455 × 62 × 28 feet.
Builders: Permanente Shipyard No. 1, Richmond, California, 1944.
Machinery: Steam turbines; single screw; service speed 16 knots.
Capacity: 900 one-class passengers.
Notes: Former freighter rebuilt as a passenger ship.

August 1944: Delivered as *Costa Rica Victory* to War Shipping Administration, U.S. flag; Victory class freighter.
1947: Sold to Dutch Government, Dutch flag for trooping; managed by Nederland Line; renamed *Groote Beer.*
1951: Rebuilt as a migrant/low fare passenger ship by Netherlands Dock Co., Amsterdam; managed by Holland-America Line.
July 1951: Left Rotterdam on maiden voyage to Quebec City and New York.
1960: Transferred to Trans-Ocean Steamship Co., Dutch flag; continued in transatlantic service; accommodation improved and reduced to 800 one-class; tonnage relisted as 9,384.
November 1962: Together with *Waterman* used to provide accommodation at Fremantle for Commonwealth Games.

December 1963: Sold to John S. Latsis Line, Greek flag; renamed *Marianna IV* for local Mediterranean and Moslem pilgrim voyages; tonnage relisted as 9,892.
June 1965: Chartered to Holland-America Line for summer student sailings between New York and Rotterdam; renamed *Groote Beer*, Greek flag.
December 1965: Migrant voyage from Piraeus to Australia but painted in Chandris Lines colors.
1966: Again chartered to Holland-America for summer crossings.
July 12, 1966: Serious collision with sand dredger *Pen Avon* off the Needles Lighthouse.
September 1966: Laid-up at Piraeus.
March 1967: Laid-up in Eleusis Bay; renamed *Marianna IV.*
June 1970: Scrapped at Eleusis.

Looking Immaculate: The *Groote Beer* at Holland-America's 5th Street pier in Hoboken. (*ALF collection*)

Waterman (1945)

Service: Summer season sailings between Rotterdam and New York or Quebec City; occasionally via Le Havre and Southampton. At other times to Australia, South Africa, Indonesia, etc.
Particulars: 9,176 gross tons; 455 × 62 × 28 feet.
Builders: Oregon Shipbuilding Corp., Portland, Oregon, 1945.
Machinery: Steam turbines; single screw; service speed 16 knots.
Capacity: 900 one-class passengers.
Notes: Former freighter rebuilt as a passenger ship.

February 1945: Delivered as *La Grande Victory* to War Shipping Administration, U.S. flag; Victory class freighter.
1947: Sold to Dutch Government, Dutch flag for trooping; managed by Royal Rotterdam Lloyd; renamed *Waterman.*
1951: Rebuilt as a migrant/low fare passenger ship.
1952: Began Rotterdam–New York sailings.
1960: Transferred to Trans-Ocean Steamship Co., Dutch flag; continued in transatlantic service; accommodation improved and reduced to 800 one-class; tonnage relisted as 9,374.
December 1963: Sold to John S. Latsis Line, Greek flag; renamed *Margarita* for local Mediterranean and Moslem pilgrim voyages; tonnage relisted as 9,892.
March 1970: Scrapped at Onomichi, Japan.

32

New Zealand Shipping Co.

Rangitiki

Service: London–Curaçao–Panama Canal–Wellington–Auckland–Panama–Curaçao–Port Everglades–Southampton–London. Occasional additional ports such as Madeira, Kingston, and Tahiti (southbound) and Bermuda (northbound).
Particulars: 16,985 gross tons; 552 × 79 × 33 feet.
Builders: John Brown & Co. Ltd., Clydebank, Scotland, 1929.
Machinery: Doxford type diesels; twin screw; service speed 16 knots.
Capacity: 121 first class and 284 tourist class.

August 29, 1928: Launched.
February 15, 1929: Departed from Southampton on maiden voyage to New Zealand; 100 first class, eighty-six second class, and 412 third class.
1930: Tonnage listed as 16,698.
December 1940: Refitted as troop transport for British Ministry of War Transport.
1947–48: Restored and refitted for resumption of passenger service to New Zealand; original Sulzer diesels replaced with Doxford diesels.
September 24, 1948 24 Sep: Left London on first post-war voyage to New Zealand.
September 1961: First voyage Port Everglades–Southampton.
June 1962: Final voyage Port Everglades–Southampton.
1962: Scrapped at Santander, Spain.

Rangitata

Service: London–Curaçao–Panama Canal–Wellington–Auckland–Panama–Curaçao–Port Everglades–Southampton–London. Occasional additional ports such as Madeira, Kingston, and Tahiti (southbound) and Bermuda (northbound).
Particulars: 16,969 gross tons; 552 × 79 × 33 feet.
Builders: John Brown & Co. Ltd., Clydebank, Scotland, 1929.
Machinery: Doxford type diesels; twin screw; service speed 16 knots.
Capacity: 123 first class and 288 tourist class.

March 26, 1929: Launched.
November 22, 1929: Departed from Southampton on maiden voyage to Wellington.
February 1941: Refitted as troop transport for British Ministry of War Shipping.
1948–49: Restored and refitted for resumption of passenger service to New Zealand; original Sulzer diesels replaced with Doxford diesels.
September 23, 1949: Left London on post-war maiden voyage to New Zealand.
November 1961: First sailing Port Everglades–Southampton.
April 1962: Final voyage Port Everglades–Southampton.
1962: Sold to Dutch shipbreakers; then resold to Yugoslav breakers; renamed *Rang.*
July 21, 1962: Arrived at Split to be scrapped.

Rangitoto

Service: London–Curaçao–Panama Canal–Wellington–Auckland–Panama–Curaçao–Port Everglades–Southampton–London. Occasional additional ports such as Madeira, Kingston and Tahiti (southbound) and Bermuda (northbound).
Particulars: 21,809 gross tons; 609 × 78 × 32 feet.
Builders: Vickers-Armstrong Shipbuilders Ltd., Newcastle, England, 1949.
Machinery: Doxford type diesels; twin screw; service speed 16½ knots.
Capacity: 436 one-class passengers.
January 12, 1949: Launched.

Above: Pre-War Design: The twin-funnel *Rangitata* in London's Royal Docks. (*Kenneth Wrightman collection, courtesy of Mick Lindsay*)

Right: The *Rangitoto* dressed in flags on a rare visit to Melbourne. (*Tim Noble collection*)

August 25, 1949: Left London on maiden voyage to Wellington.
1961: First voyage Port Everglades–London.
1965: Mainmast removed.
1966: Repainted in Federal Steam Navigation Co. colors.
July 1969: Withdrawn; laid-up.
August 1969: Sold to Oriental South America Line (C. Y. Tung Group), Liberian flag; renamed *Oriental Carnaval.* Refitted for 300 first class passengers; tonnage relisted as 19,567.
December 2, 1970: Departed from San Francisco on first eastbound around-the-world voyage for Orient Overseas Line.
May 9, 1974: Ended Orient Overseas Line world voyages.
March 7, 1975: Laid-up at Hong Kong.
February 1976: Demolition commenced at Hong Kong by Lee Sing Shipbreaking Co.

Rangitane

Service: London–Curaçao–Panama Canal–Wellington–Auckland–Panama–Curaçao–Port Everglades–Southampton–London. Occasional additional ports such as Madeira, Kingston, and Tahiti (southbound) and Bermuda (northbound).
Particulars: 21,867 gross tons; 609 × 78 × 32 feet.
Builders: Vickers-Armstrong Shipbuilders Ltd., Newcastle, England, 1949.
Machinery: Doxford type diesels; twin screw; service speed 16½ knots.
Capacity: 436 one-class passengers.

June 30, 1949: Launched.
January 27, 1950: Left London on maiden voyage to Wellington.
February 1956: Engine trouble off Panama; later to Glasgow for repairs.
October 1957: Collided with freighter *Hawaiian Tourist* while in the Panama Canal.
February 1961: First voyage Port Everglades–Southampton.
1965: Mainmast removed.
1966: Repainted in Federal Steam Navigation Co. colors.
April 1968: Final voyage Port Everglades-Southampton; completed forty-seven round voyages to New Zealand.
May 6, 1968: Withdrawn; laid-up. Later sold to Astroguarda Compañía Navegación, Greek flag; renamed *Jan*; one outward voyage to Kaohsiung, presumably to be scrapped.
September 11, 1968: Arrived at Kaohsiung; laid-up.
January 1969: Sold to Oriental Latin America Lines (C. Y. Tung Group), Liberian flag; renamed *Oriental Esmeralda.* Refitted for 300 first class passengers; tonnage relisted as 19,567.
June 4, 1969: Departed from San Diego on first eastbound around-the-world voyage for Orient Overseas Line.
May 9, 1974: Ended Orient Overseas Line world voyages.
March 7, 1975: Laid-up at Hong Kong.
April 2, 1976: Arrived at Kaohsiung and broken-up by I. Shing Steel & Iron Works.

Ruahine

Service: London–Curaçao–Panama Canal–Wellington–Auckland–Panama–Curaçao–Port Everglades–Southampton–London. Occasional additional ports such as Madeira, Kingston, and Tahiti (southbound) and Bermuda (northbound).
Particulars: 17,851 gross tons; 584 × 75 × 29 feet.
Builders: John Brown & Co. Ltd., Clydebank, Scotland, 1951.

The handsome, big combo liner *Rangitane* seen passing Gravesend. (*Mick Lindsay collection*)

Machinery: Doxford diesels; twin screw; service speed 16½ knots.
Capacity: 267 one-class passengers.
December 11, 1950: Launched.
May 22, 1951: Left London on maiden voyage to Wellington.
August 1961: First voyage: Port Everglades–Southampton.
1965: Mainmast removed.
1966: Repainted in Federal Steam Navigation Co. colors.
1967: Transferred to Federal Steam Navigation Co.
July 1968: Final voyage: Port Everglades–London; later withdrawn from service; laid-up. Later sold to International Export Lines (C. Y. Tung Group), Bahamian flag; renamed *Oriental Rio*. Later transferred to Chinese Maritime Trust (also C. Y. Tung Group), Taiwanese flag; operated by Orient Overseas Line. Refitted; tonnage relisted as 17,730; accommodation restyled for 220 all-first class passengers.
December 31, 1973: Arrived at Kaohsiung for scrapping.

Remuera

Service: London–Curaçao–Panama Canal–Wellington–Auckland–Panama–Curaçao–Port Everglades–Southampton–London. Occasional additional ports such as Madeira, Kingston, and Tahiti (southbound) and Bermuda (northbound).
Particulars: 13,619 gross tons; 531 × 70 × 30 feet.
Builders: Harland & Wolff Ltd., Belfast, Northern Ireland, 1948.
Machinery: Steam turbines; twin screw; service speed 18 knots.
Capacity: 350 one-class passengers.

1948–61: Sailed as *Parthia* for Cunard Line, British flag (qv).
September 23, 1961: Departed from Liverpool on final voyage to New York.
November 1961: Considered for purchase by H. C. Sleigh & Co., Australian flag, for Australia-Japan service, but failed to materialize. Sold to New Zealand Shipping Co., also British flag; renamed *Remuera*; major refit at Glasgow; mainmast removed.
June 1, 1962: Left London on maiden voyage to Wellington
July 1962: First voyage Port Everglades–Southampton.
October 1964: Final voyage Port Everglades–Southampton.
November 19, 1964: Completed final New Zealand Shipping Co. voyage; sold to Eastern & Australian Steamship Co. Ltd., British flag; renamed *Aramac*; refitted at Hong Kong.
February 8, 1965: Departed Melbourne on maiden voyage to Sydney, Manila, Hong Kong, and Japanese ports.
November 22, 1969: Arrived at Kaohsiung for scrapping.
March 5, 1970: Demolition commenced.
May 31, 1970: Demolition completed.

The former *Parthia*, the *Remuera* is being refitted while in London's Royal Docks. (*Mick Lindsay collection*)

33

North German Lloyd

Berlin

Service: Bremerhaven to New York; occasionally via Southampton and Halifax (westbound only). In later years, annual sailing to Quebec City and Montreal. Also cruising from New York and Bremerhaven.
Particulars: 18,600 gross tons; 590 × 29 feet.
Builders: Sir W. G. Armstrong-Whitworth & Co., Newcastle, England, 1925.
Machinery: B&W type diesels; twin screw; service speed 16½ knots.
Capacity: 98 first class and 876 tourist class.
Notes: The first German liner on the North Atlantic since 1939.

1925–54: Sailed as *Gripsholm* for Swedish American Line (qv).
February 1, 1954: Began sailing from Bremen-America Line (partnership of Swedish American Line and North German Lloyd).
January 8, 1955: Maiden sailing from Bremerhaven as Berlin for North German Lloyd.
November 26, 1966: Arrived at La Spezia, Italy for scrapping; sold to shipbreakers for $500,000.

Bremen

Service: Bremerhaven–Southampton–Cherbourg–New York; winter cruises from New York to the Caribbean; occasional cruises from Bremerhaven.
Particulars: 32,336 gross tons; 697 × 88 × 30 feet.
Builders: Chantiers de l'Atlantique, Saint-Nazaire, France, 1939.
Machinery: Steam turbines; quadruple screw; service speed 23 knots.
Capacity: 216 first class and 906 tourist class.
Notes: West Germany's largest post-war liner to date.

February 15, 1938: Launched as *Pasteur* for Compagnie Sud-Atlantique, French flag; intended for Bordeaux–East Coast of South America service.
September 1939: Intended maiden voyage canceled owing to threat of war in Europe.
September 1939–May 1940: Laid-up for safety.
1940–46: Used as a troopship by British Ministry of War Transport; managed by Cunard-White Star.
1946–56: Peacetime trooping for French Government; mostly sailing to Indochina; capacity 4,000.
January 25, 1957: Laid-up at Brest; later considered to be refitted for Le Havre–New York service for French Line; never materialized.
September 1957: Purchased by North German Lloyd, West German flag; renamed *Bremen*; sailed Brest–Bremerhaven to be rebuilt.
1957–59: Thoroughly rebuilt; tonnage increased from 29,253 to 32,336.
July 9, 1959: Departed Bremerhaven on maiden voyage to New York.
1971: Mostly cruising.
December 1971: Sold to Chandris Cruises, Greek flag for $3 million; renamed *Regina Magna*; cruising only.
May 1972: Maiden Chandris cruise: Amsterdam–Scandinavia.
October 17, 1974: Laid-up in Perama Bay, Greece.
1977: Sold to Philippine Singapore Ports Corp, Philippines flag.
October 6, 1977: Left Piraeus under tow for Jeddah for use as an accommodation ship for 3,600 refinery and construction workers; renamed *Saudi Phil I.*
November 1, 1977: Arrived at Jeddah.
1978: Renamed *Filipinas Saudi I.*
April 1980: Sold for scrapping on Taiwan.
June 9, 1980: Sank while empty and being towed from Jeddah to Kaohsiung.

Summer morning departure in July 1955—the *Berlin* with the *Île de France* beyond. The *Franconia*, *Queen Elizabeth*, and *Andrea Doria* are still at berth. (*Port Authority of New York & New Jersey*)

The rebuilt *Bremen* arriving in the lower Hudson River. (*Author's collection*)

Changing Flags: The *Bremen* in a subsequent career as the Greek cruise ship *Regina Magna*. (*ALF collection*)

The *Europa* (ex-*Kungsholm*) calling at Southampton. (*Mick Lindsay collection*)

Europa (1953)

Service: Bremerhaven–Southampton–Cherbourg–New York; considerable cruising from New York, Bremerhaven and Genoa.
Particulars: 21,514 gross tons; 600 × 77 × 26 feet.
Builders: De Schelde Shipyard, Flushing, Holland, 1953.
Machinery: B&W type diesels; twin screw; service speed 19 knots.
Capacity: 122 first class and 721 tourist class; later changed to 769 one-class.
1953–65: Sailed as *Kungsholm* for Swedish American Line, Swedish flag (qv).
October 15, 1965: Transferred at Gothenburg to North German Lloyd, West German flag.
November 1965: Renamed *Europa*; refitted.
January 9, 1966: Departed from Bremerhaven on maiden voyage to New York.
1970: North German Lloyd merged with Hamburg America Line to form Hapag-Lloyd; hull and funnels repainted.
1971: Transatlantic service discontinued; year-round cruising hereafter.
October 1981: Sold to Independent Continental Lines (Costa Group), Panama flag; renamed *Columbus C*. Mostly European cruises.
July 29, 1984: Struck breakwater and badly damaged while entering Cadiz and then later sank at her berth.
September 1984: Declared a complete loss.
November 1984: Refloated.
March 1985: Sold for scrap; towed to Barcelona and demolished.

34

Norwegian America Line

Stavangerfjord

Service: Oslo–Copenhagen–Kristiansand–Bergen–New York; occasionally including Halifax (westbound only).
Particulars: 14,015 gross tons; 553 × 64 × 27 feet.
Builders: Cammell Laird & Co., Birkenhead, England, 1918.
Machinery: Steam quadruple-expansion turbines; twin screw; service speed 16½ knots.
Capacity: 122 first class, 222 cabin class, and 335 tourist class; after 1956: ninety first class, 172 cabin class, and 413 tourist class.

May 21, 1917: Launched.
April 1918: Completed; moved from Birkenhead to New York for safety.
September 1918: Maiden voyage: Oslo–Bergen–New York; 12,977 gross tons; eighty-eight first class, 318 second class, and 820 third class.

The stately *Stavangerfjord* departing from a lower East River pier at New York in 1946. (*ALF collection*)

1924: Converted from coal to oil burning.
1931: Accommodation restyled as 147 first class, 207 tourist class, and 820 third class.
1938: Passenger accommodation modernized.
December 30, 1939: Arrived at Oslo; laid-up owing to war in Europe.
1940–45: Used as Nazi troop depot ship; never sailed during the war.
August 1945: First peacetime commercial Atlantic liner sailing after the war; tonnage relisted as 13,156.
December 1953: Damaged and lost rudder during Atlantic storm.
November–December 1956: Major refit; tonnage relisted as 14,015; passenger accommodation altered.
December 14, 1963: Final arrival at Oslo, having steamed 2.8 million miles, made 770 Atlantic crossings, carried 500,000 passengers and reached forty-five years of age. Later sold to Hong Kong scrappers for $420,000.
February 2, 1964: Arrived at Hong Kong for scrapping.

Oslofjord

Service: Oslo–Copenhagen–Kristiansand–Stavanger–Bergen–New York; considerable cruising.
Particulars: 16,844 gross tons; 577 × 72 × 26 feet.
Builders: Netherlands Shipbuilding Co., Amsterdam, Holland, 1949.
Machinery: Stork type diesels; twin screw; service speed 20 knots.
Capacity: 179 first class and 467 tourist class; 360 one-class for cruises.

April 2, 1949: Launched by HRH Crown Princess Martha of Norway.
November 26, 1949: Left Oslo on maiden voyage to New York.

February 1957: Almost flooded and capsized while in dry dock at Bethlehem Steel shipyard, Hoboken, New Jersey.
November–December 1957: Refit.
June 1966: Proposed sale to Finnlines, Finnish flag; never materialized.
November 3, 1966: Arrived at Amsterdam for three-month refit; made more suitable for cruising; tonnage relisted as 16,923.
December 22, 1967: Began charter to Greek Line for cruises from Southampton.
September 1968: Proposed charter to Ensco Shipping Co., British flag; Liverpool–Montreal service during summer 1969; scheme never materialized.
October 1968: Commenced three-year charter to Costa Line: Mediterranean cruises from Genoa in summer; Caribbean cruises from San Juan in winter.

Troubles: The *Oslofjord* slipped off the dry dock blocks at the Bethlehem Steel shipyard in Hoboken on a winter's morning in 1957. (*Hoboken Historical Museum*)

Smart Lines: The *Oslofjord* at Southampton while under charter to the Greek Line. (*Mick Lindsay collection*)

December 1969: Renamed *Fulvia* by Costa.
July 20, 1970: Sank off Tenerife after being abandoned following fire.

Bergensfjord

Service: Oslo–Copenhagen–Kristiansand–Stavanger–Bergen–New York; considerable off-season cruising.
Particulars: 18,739 gross tons; 578 × 72 × 27 feet.
Builders: Swan, Hunter & Wigham Richardson Ltd., Wallsend-on-Tyne, England, 1956.
Machinery: Stork type diesels; twin screw; service speed 20 knots.
Capacity: 126 first class and 752 tourist class; 420 one-class for cruising.

June 1, 1954: Keel laid.
July 18, 1955: Launched by HRH Princess Astrid of Norway.
May 30, 1956: Left Oslo on maiden voyage to New York.
April 1971: Unexpectedly sold to French Line to replace *Antilles*.
November 1971: Delivered to French Line, French flag; renamed *De Grasse* (original intention was *Louisianne*). Refitted at Le Havre; 580 one-class passengers; Le Havre–West Indies service and cruising.
September 1973: Reportedly sold to Home Lines for $13½ million; never materialized. Then reported as sold to Coral Riviera Ltd., Israeli flag for use as floating hotel at Tel Aviv; again never materialized.
November 1973: Sold to Thoresen & Co. Ltd., Singapore flag; renamed *Rasa Sayang*; refitted.
November 1974: Commenced Singapore–Indonesia cruise service for Rasa Sayang Cruises.
June 2, 1977: Damaged by fire while at sea; abandoned by passengers and crew.
June 4, 1977: Towed to Singapore; later repaired.
June 19, 1978: Laid-up; offered for sale.
December 11, 1978: Arrived at Piraeus after being sold to Sunlit Cruises Ltd., Cypriot flag; renamed *Golden Moon*; laid-up in Perama Bay.
May 1979: Charter to Dutch travel firm for cruises from Rotterdam; intended to be renamed *Prins van Oranje*; never materialized.
July 1980: Sold to other Greek owners, to Greek Aphrodite Maritime Co.; renamed *Rasa Sayang* for use by CTC Lines for cruising from Sydney.
August 27, 1980: Destroyed by fire at Kynosoura; towed offshore, run aground, and then capsized; later demolished on the site.

Launch of the new Norwegian America flagship, the *Bergensfjord*. (*Cronican-Arroyo collection*)

The *Bergensfjord* but seen in her next life as French Line's *De Grasse*. (*Mick Lindsay collection*)

Sagafjord

Service: Some Oslo–Copenhagen–Bergen–New York sailings; 1966–68: Annual transatlantic positioning voyages to/from New York and Port Everglades. Mostly cruising.
Particulars: 24,002 gross tons; 615 × 82 × 27 feet.
Builders: Société des Forges et Chantiers de la Méditerranée, Toulon, France, 1965.
Machinery: Sulzer diesels; twin screw; service speed 20 knots.
Capacity: Seventy first class and 719 tourist class; mostly about 500 one-class for cruising.

June 13, 1964: Launched; intended name was *Norway*.
October 2, 1965: Left Oslo on maiden voyage to New York; ship owned 60 percent by Norwegian America Line and 40 percent by Leif Högh & Co., both Norwegian flag.
November 1976–March 1977: Temporarily laid-up.
1980: Reregistered to Norwegian America Cruises.
September 1980–January 1981: Major refit costing $12 million by Blohm & Voss Shipyard, Hamburg; addition of top deck; change in engines; fifteen cabins added. Capacity relisted as 509.
May 1983: Sold to Cunard Line, Bahamian flag; marketed as Cunard-Norwegian America Cruises. Plan to rename *Sagafjord* and *Vistafjord* as *Mauretania* and *Aquitania* never materialized.
1990: Operation changed to Cunard with title Cunard-Norwegian America/NAC being dropped.
February 26, 1996: Breakdown in the Philippines during world cruise; later repaired at Singapore.
July 1996: Began brief charter to Germany's Transocean Tours; renamed *Gripsholm*; later grounded near Copenhagen, but refloated and repaired.
1997: Sold to Saga Cruises, Bahamian flag; renamed *Saga Rose*.
May 1997: First Saga cruise from Dover.
July 29, 1999: Collision with trawler off Norwegian coast.
2000: Capacity listed as 587.
October 2009: Withdrawn from cruise service.
February 2010: At Gibraltar with plans to become accommodation and stores ship; never materialized.
April 2010: Sailed to South Africa with rumors of becoming a hotel; later to East Africa.
May 23, 2010: Reached Taiwan with rumors of heading for Japan.
May 27, 2010: Reached Shanghai; later moved to Jiangyin.
May 29, 2010: At Jiangyin for scrapping by Changjiang Ship Recycling Co.

The beautiful *Sagafjord* berthed at Southampton (*Mick Lindsay collection*)

Seen at New York but in Cunard colors and across from the *Song of Norway*. (*Author's collection*)

35

Oranje Line

Prins Willem van Oranje

Service: Rotterdam–Montreal (to Halifax and St. John NB in winter); after 1959, extended to Chicago, Toronto, and other Great Lakes ports.
Particulars: 7,328 gross tons; 462 × 62 × 25 feet.
Builders: Boele's Shipbuilding & Engineering Co., Bolnes, Holland, 1953.
Machinery: Werkspoor-Lugt diesel; single screw; service speed 17 knots.
Capacity: Sixty one-class passengers.
Notes: Ice-strengthened hull.

September 1953: Maiden voyage: Rotterdam–Montreal via Antwerp.
June 1959: Began using St. Lawrence Seaway and sailing to Toronto, Chicago, and other Great Lakes ports.
1964: Reduced to twelve passengers.
February 1965: Sold to V. E. B. Deutsche Seereederei, East German flag; for £500,000; renamed *Ferdinand Freiligrath.*
1974: Renamed *Freijo* for unidentified new owners; then resold to Universal Shipping Corp Inc., Panamanian flag; renamed *Universal Honolulu*. General tramping services.
1976: Renamed *August 8th.*
October 1, 1977: Laid-up at Singapore.
April 20, 1979: Arrived in tow at Kaohsiung; later scrapped.

Prinses Irene

Service: North Europe–Canada–U.S. Great Lakes ports (same as *Prins Willem van Oranje*); but in winter, to Gulf of Mexico ports (Vera Cruz, Tampico, etc.).
Particulars: 8,526 gross tons; 456 × 61 × 28 feet.

The combo liner *Prins Willem van Oranje*. (*Nico Guns collection*)

Builders: De Merwede Shipbuilding Co., Hardinxveld, Holland, 1959.
Machinery: MAN type diesels; single screw; service speed 17 knots.
Capacity: 116 one-class passengers.

July 12, 1958: Launched by HRH Princess Irene of the Netherlands.
April 29, 1959: Departed Rotterdam on maiden voyage to Montreal.
June 10, 1959: Took part in opening of St. Lawrence Seaway; commenced extended service to Chicago, etc.
1964: Chartered to Cunard Line for freighter service from Glasgow and Liverpool to New York and other U.S. East Coast ports.
December 1964: Sold to Verolme Shipyard, Dutch flag; then resold to Djakarta Lloyd, Indonesian flag; renamed *Tjut Nyak Dhien*; rebuilt with 900 passenger berths; often used in Moslem pilgrim trade from Jakarta to Jeddah.
1979: Transferred to Indonesian Navy; renamed *Tanjung Oisina*; refitted as a troop transport.
2013: Scrapped in Indonesia.

Prinses Margriet

Service: North Europe-Canada-U.S. Great Lakes ports (same as *Prins Willem van Oranje*).
Particulars: 9,336 gross tons; 456 × 61 × 28 feet.
Builders: De Merwede Shipbuilding Co., Hardinxveld, Holland, 1961.
Machinery: MAN type diesel; single screw; service speed 17 knots.
Capacity: 111 one-class passengers.
Notes: Ice-strengthened hull.

December 10, 1960: Launched by HRH Crown Princess Beatrix as Princess Margriet was ill at the time.
July 1961: Maiden voyage from Rotterdam to Montreal, Chicago, etc.
December 1964: Sold to Holland-America Line (qv).

Oranje Line's *Prinses Margriet* was unique—she serviced the Great Lakes. (*ALF collection*)

36

P&O-Orient Lines

Orcades

Service: Periodically Southampton–Port Everglades via Cherbourg, Bermuda and/or Nassau (and usually extended to Los Angeles, San Francisco, Victoria, and Vancouver) as part of worldwide and U.K.–Australia passenger sailings. Also cruising.
Particulars: 28,396 gross tons; 709 × 90 × 30 feet.
Builders: Vickers-Armstrong Shipbuilders Ltd., Barrow-in-Furness, England, 1948.
Machinery: Steam turbines; twin screw; service speed 22 knots.
Capacity: 631 first class and 734 tourist class.

October 14, 1947: Launched; construction delayed by labor problems and material shortages; cost $9 million.
November 1948: During trials reached 24.74 knots.
December 14, 1948: Departed Tilbury on maiden voyage to Australia; cut passage time between London and Sydney from thirty-six to twenty-eight days.
May 7, 1952: Aground in Port Philip Bay.
December 1954: First voyage across the Pacific to North American West Coast.
August 22, 1955: Departed Southampton on first voyage to Australia via Panama.
November 1956: Used for two weeks as floating hotel at Melbourne during Olympic Games.
January–February 1959: Extensive refit at Belfast.
May 1960: Transferred from Orient Line to P&O-Orient Lines, both British flag.
May 1964: Repainted in all-white hull replacing original corn-colored hull; converted to 1,635 all one-class passengers.
October 1966: Transferred from P&O-Orient Lines to P&O Line.
June 23, 1970: Damaged in storm while off Fremantle.
April 17, 1972: Boiler room fire while at Hong Kong; spare parts sent out from Southampton from laid-up *Iberia.*
October 13, 1972: Laid-up at Southampton.
January 1973: Departed Southampton with small crew bound for Kaohsiung.
March 15, 1973: Demolition began at Kaohsiung.

Himalaya

Service: Worldwide itineraries including trans-Atlantic crossings (same as *Orcades).*
Particulars: 27,955 gross tons; 709 × 91 × 31 feet.
Builders: Vickers-Armstrong Shipbuilders Ltd., Barrow-in-Furness, England, 1949.
Machinery: Steam turbines; twin screw; service speed 22 knots.
Capacity: 758 first class and 401 tourist class.

March 1945: Ordered.
February 1946: Keel laid.
October 5, 1948: Launched; cost from $4.8 million to $6.8 million; eighteenth-month delay in completion owing to shortage of parts, labor difficulties and high demands on post-war British shipyards.
August 1949: Departed Barrow; then dry docked at Belfast; managed over 25 knots on trials. P&O's largest liner yet.
October 6, 1949: Departed from Tilbury on first voyage to Australia, cutting time London–Melbourne from thirty-eight to twenty-eight days.
July–August 1950: Made two U.K.–Mediterranean cruises, first for P&O since 1939.
December 1954: First cruise from Sydney.
August 30, 1956: Onboard explosion; four crewmembers killed.
February 1958: Inaugurated new joint service with Orient Line and known as Orient & Pacific Lines to North American West Coast ports.
February 1959: Inaugurated North American West Coast–Japan service.

Orient Line's first post-war liner, the *Orcades,* seen berthed at Melbourne. (*Tim Noble collection*)

The splendid looking *Himalaya* was one of P&O-Orient's most popular liners. (*Tim Noble collection*)

June 1959: Fitted with stabilizers.
November 1959: Refit at Rotterdam and given complete air-conditioning; accommodation changed to 667 first class, 405 tourist, and seventy-eight interchangeable berths.
May 1960: Formation of P&O-Orient Lines.
November 1963: During refit at Tilbury restyled for 1,416 one-class passengers; tonnage relisted as 27,989.
1969: Tonnage relisted as 28,047.
October 1969: Final P&O liner sailing from Tilbury; thereafter all sailings from Southampton.
May 16, 1974: Final departure from Southampton.
October 18, 1974: Departed Sydney on final voyage: One-way cruise to Hong Kong.
November 28, 1974: Arrived at Kaohsiung to be scrapped by Tong Cheng Steel Manufacturing Co. Ltd.

Chusan

Service: Worldwide itineraries, including transatlantic crossings (same as Orcades).
Particulars: 24,215 gross tons; 672 × 85 × 29 feet.
Builders: Vickers-Armstrong Shipbuilders Ltd., Barrow-in-Furness, England, 1950.
Machinery: Steam turbines; twin screw; service speed 22 knots.
Capacity: 475 first class and 551 tourist class.
February 1947: Keel laid; delayed in construction.
June 28, 1949: Launched; P&O's largest liner ever for London–Far East service.
May 1950: Delivered; first large passenger ship to be fitted with Denny-Brown fin stabilizers.
June 1950: Made short cruise to Rotterdam for International Freight Conference; then four cruises.
September 1950: Maiden line voyage: London–Bombay.
November 1950: Maiden voyage to Hong Kong.
May 1952: Fitted with Thorneycroft smoke-deflecting top to her funnel.
June 12, 1953: Collided with Harrison Line freighter *Prospector* in thick fog in English Channel; *Chusan* damaged.
April 1954: Made P&O's first post-war calls in Japan.
April 1959: Made P&O's first around-the-world line voyage.
December 1959: Refit at Belfast: Full air-conditioning installed; accommodation modernized; berthing rearranged for 464 first class and 541 tourist class; tonnage relisted as 24,261.
June 1963: Reassigned to London–Australia service; first call at Sydney.
1969: Cruising mostly.
1970: Made final P&O line voyage Bombay–London.
1971–73: Charter cruises from Cape Town, including visit to New York in October 1971.
April 5, 1973: Final arrival at Southampton.
May 12, 1973: Departed Southampton via Cape Town for Kaohsiung to be scrapped; demolition begun July 1973.

Three Liners at Melbourne: The *Oronsay* (left), the *Fairstar* (middle), and the *Australis*. (*Tim Noble collection*)

Oronsay

Service: Worldwide itineraries, including transatlantic crossings (same as *Orcades*).
Particulars: 27,632 gross tons; 709 × 90 × 30 feet.
Builders: Vickers-Armstrong Shipbuilders Ltd., Barrow-in-Furness, England, 1951.
Machinery: Steam turbines; twin screw; service speed 22 knots.
Capacity: 612 first class and 804 tourist class.

June 30, 1950: Launched; cost $9.6 million.
October 28–31, 1950: Serious fire while fitting-out; fire raged for three days; ship partially flooded; completion delayed by two months.
May 1951: Maiden voyage from Tilbury to Australia.
January 1, 1954: Opened new P&O-Orient experimental service northward from Sydney and Auckland to Vancouver and San Francisco.
1959: Major refit; modernized.
1960: Transferred from Orient Line to P&O-Orient Lines.
1964: Repainted in all-white hull.
1966: Transferred from P&O-Orient Lines to P&O Lines.
January 14–February 4, 1970: Idle at Vancouver owing to outbreak of typhoid.
September 1975: Withdrawn from service at Hong Kong.
October 7, 1975: Arrived at Kaohsiung for scrapping.
April 10, 1976: Demolition begun.

Arcadia

Service: Worldwide itineraries, including transatlantic crossings (same as *Orcades*).
Particulars: 29,734 gross tons; 721 × 91 × 30 feet.
Builders: John Brown & Co. Ltd., Clydebank, Scotland, 1954.
Machinery: Steam turbines; twin screw; service speed 22 knots.
Capacity: 655 first class and 735 tourist class.

June 28, 1951: Keel laid; construction delayed because of steel shortages, etc.
May 14, 1953: Launched; Orient Line's *Orsova* launched on the same day but at Barrow.
January 1954: During sea trials reached 24.7 knots.
February 22, 1954: Departed Tilbury on maiden voyage to Australia.
May–October 1954: Made nine cruises.
October 25, 1954: Departing Tilbury Landing Stage and wanting to avoid a collision with the nearby *Orcades*, *Arcadia* rammed and sank the tug *Cervia*.
April 1, 1959: Arrived at Belfast for major refit: Given full air-conditioning and modernized accommodation.
September 1959: Visit to New York as part of a three-week cruise from Southampton.
1960: Transferred to P&O-Orient Lines.
1966: Transferred to P&O Lines.
April 1970: During refit at Southampton, mainmast removed and foremast shortened.
May 1970: Began summer season series of cruises from San Francisco to Alaska and British Columbia.
1973: Converted to 1,372 one-class passengers.
1974: Used mostly for cruises from Sydney.
May 1976: Final voyage from Southampton; fulltime Australian cruising.
January 29, 1979: Final departure from Sydney; cruise to Singapore.
February 22, 1979: Arrived at Kaohsiung to be scrapped.
February 28, 1979: Demolition began by Lee Chong Steel & Iron Works.

Above: The beautiful *Arcadia*. (*Anton Logvinenko*)

Right: The *Arcadia* as seen from the Sydney Harbor Bridge in February 1972. (*Frank Andrews*)

Iberia

Service: Worldwide itineraries, including transatlantic crossings (same as *Orcades).*
Particulars: 29,614 gross tons; 719 × 91 × 30 feet.
Builders: Harland & Wolff Ltd., Belfast, Northern Ireland, 1954.
Machinery: Steam turbines; twin screw; service speed 22 knots.
Capacity: 673 first class and 733 tourist class.

January 21, 1954: Launched.
September 28, 1954: Departed Tilbury on maiden voyage to Australia.
June 1955: Began series of six summer season cruises from Southampton.
March 27, 1956: Badly damaged in heavy weather off Ceylon when rammed by the American tanker *Stanvac Pretoria*; *Iberia* had an 80-foot-long gash in her port side. Repairs at Colombo and full repairs at Sydney.
June 1959: Only visit to New York as part of a three-week cruise from Southampton.
January 1960: First cruise from Sydney.
January–March 1961: Refit at Southampton; cost $1 million; given full air-conditioning; modernization of accommodation.
October 17, 1961: Complete electrical breakdown off Auckland. Noted for both mechanical and stability problems for most of her P&O career—overall, said to be an "unlucky ship."
June 1966: Turbine troubles between Kobe and Yokohama.
1968: Further turbine problems.
October–November 1969: Most troubled voyage: funnel caught fire at Pago Pago; electrical failure at Honolulu; engine trouble off Acapulco; and fuel leak at Curaçao.
December 1969: Repairs and refit; mainmast removed.
September 1971: Refit.
April 19, 1972: Completed final P&O voyage; laid-up at Southampton; only eighteen years of service; later sold to Mitsui & Co. for demolition.
June 28, 1972: Left Southampton bound for Taiwan scrapyards.
September 5, 1972: Arrived Kaohsiung after ten-week voyage; handed over to Tung Cheng Steel Corp.

Orsova

Service: Worldwide itineraries, including transatlantic crossings (same as *Orcades*).
Particulars: 28,790 gross tons; 723 × 90 × 30 feet.
Builders: Vickers-Armstrong Shipbuilders Ltd., Barrow-in-Furness, England, 1954.
Machinery: Steam turbines; twin screw; service speed 22 knots.
Capacity: 694 first class and 809 tourist class.

The beautiful, but long-troubled *Iberia*. (*Mick Lindsay collection*)

Two Liners at Naples: The *Orsova* (front) and the *Conte Biancamano* (behind). (*Tim Noble collection*)

The mast-less *Orsova* docked at San Francisco. (*Mick Lindsay collection*)

The mighty *Oriana* passes through the Panama Canal. (*Mick Lindsay collection*)

May 14, 1953: Launched; same day as *Arcadia* of P&O.
March 17, 1954: Departed Tilbury on her maiden voyage to Australia.
April 1955: First around-the-world voyage; voyage completed in July, covering 44,000 miles.
1960: Major refit at Newcastle; modernized. Also transferred from Orient Line to P&O-Orient Lines.
May 1964: Hull coloring changed to all white.
1966: Transferred from P&O-Orient Lines to P&O Lines.
November 25, 1972: Began refit at Southampton.
November 25, 1973: Completed final P&O sailing; laid-up at Southampton.
February 14, 1974: Arrived at Kaohsiung for scrapping.
December 17, 1974: Demolition begun.

Oriana

Service: Worldwide itineraries, including transatlantic crossings (same as *Orcades*).
Particulars: 41,923 gross tons; 804 × 97 × 31 feet.
Builders: Vickers-Armstrong Shipbuilders Ltd., Barrow-in-Furness, England, 1960.
Machinery: Steam turbines; twin screw; service speed 27½ knots.
Capacity: 638 first class and 1,496 tourist class.
Notes: The largest liner built in England and fastest liner in U.K.–Australia service.

November 3, 1959: Launched by HRH Princess Alexandra; ordered by Orient Line, but completed for P&O-Orient Lines.
December 3, 1960: Departed from Southampton on maiden voyage to Sydney; passage time reduced from four to three weeks.
December 3, 1962: Collision off Los Angeles with U.S. Navy aircraft carrier USS *Kearsage*.
March 1964: Record-making passage between Auckland Sydney at 27.76 knots.
1966: Transferred to P&O Lines.
June 17, 1970: Boiler fire.
August 11, 1970: Engine room fire in Southampton Water off Fawley.
1973: Cruising only; transferred to P&O Cruises Ltd.; 1,700 one-class passengers; tonnage relisted as 41,915.
August 10, 1979: Departed Southampton on maiden transatlantic cruise: Southampton–Reykjavik–Corner Brook–Halifax–Boston–New York–Southampton.
October 1981: Final Southampton–Sydney voyage.
December 1981: Assigned to fulltime cruise service from Sydney.
March 14, 1986: Departed on final cruise from Sydney.
May 1986: Sold to Daiwa Group, Japanese flag.
June 1986: Towed from Sydney to Beppu Bay for use as floating hotel, museum, and entertainment center; unsuccessful.
July 1995: Sold to Chinese buyers for use as a floating hotel at Qinhuangdao.
November 1998: Moved to Shanghai.
September 2000: Auctioned off.
June 2002: Moved to Dalian; later opened as hotel, museum, and entertainment center.
June 2004: Heavily damaged by typhoon and later capsized at her berth; later salvaged but beyond repair.
May 2005: Towed to Zhangjiagang for scrapping.

A symbol of great 1950s design, the *Canberra* was a very popular liner. (*Mick Lindsay collection*)

Canberra (1961)

Service: Worldwide itineraries, including transatlantic crossings (same as *Orcades*).
Particulars: 45,733 gross tons; 818 × 102 × 32 feet.
Builders: Harland & Wolff Ltd., Belfast, Northern Ireland, 1961.
Machinery: Steam turbo-electric; twin screw; service speed 27½ knots.
Capacity: Adjustable 556 or 596 first class and 1,716 or 1,616 tourist class.
Notes: Largest liner of her time built for a service other than the North Atlantic.

March 16, 1960: Launched; ordered by P&O Lines, but completed for P&O-Orient Lines; cost in excess of $35 million.
May 5, 1961: Delivered to P&O.
June 2, 1961: Left Southampton on maiden voyage to Sydney and around the world.
1962–63: Some cruises to New York.
January 5, 1963: Disabled by major engine problems off Malta; forced to return to Southampton and then to Belfast for extended repairs.
1966: Transferred to P&O Lines.
February–September 1973: Transferred to P&O Cruises; 1,737 one-class passengers. Based at New York for series of seventeen cruises; unsuccessful.
February–March 1973: Temporarily laid-up at Wilmington, North Carolina.
July 12–15, 1973: Aground off Grenada; later refloated.
August 14, 1973: Aground at entrance to St. Thomas harbor; refloated.
September 1973: Considered to be prematurely withdrawn and scrapped; plans changed and ship retained.
April 9, 1982: Sailed from Southampton Falklands as a troopship.
July 11, 1982: Returned to Southampton following end of Falklands War; refitted and restored.
September 1982: Resumed cruising.
September 1997: Final P&O cruise; rumored to be sold to Premier Cruises and renamed *Constable*, but never materialized.
October 31, 1997: Beached at Gadani Beach, Pakistan, for scrapping; took one year to completely demolish.

37

Polish Ocean Lines

Batory

Service: Gdynia–Copenhagen–Southampton or London–Quebec City–Montreal. Occasional calls at Le Havre, Bremerhaven, Helsinki, and Boston. Winter cruising from London to the Canaries, West Africa, Mediterranean, and the Caribbean.
Particulars: 14,287 gross tons; 526 × 71 × 24 feet.
Builders: Cantieri Riuniti dell'Adriatico, Monfalcone, Italy, 1936.
Machinery: Sulzer diesels; twin screw; service speed 18 knots.
Capacity: Seventy-six first class and 740 tourist class.

July 3, 1935: Launched; paid for in coal shipments from Poland to Italy.
May 1936: Maiden voyage: Gdynia–New York; 370 tourist class and 400 third class passengers.
September 1939: Laid-up in Upper Hudson River off Yonkers, New York due to Nazi invasion of Poland; later transferred to British Ministry of War Transport; refitted at Glasgow for trooping.
1940–46: Trooping.
April 1946: Returned to Polish Ocean Lines; major refit at Antwerp.
1946: Damaged by fire at Antwerp shipyard.
April 1947: Returned to Gdynia–New York service.
January 1951: Withdrawn from transatlantic service as a result of a series of political and labor problems, the most serious being the escape of a Communist spy aboard the ship. Ship sent to Hebburn-on-Tyne, England for major refit; repainted in grey hull.
August 1951: Commenced new, alternative service: Gdynia–Southampton–Gibraltar–Malta–Suez–Aden–Karachi–Bombay; also occasional cruising.
January–August 1957: Refit at Bremerhaven; accommodation changed to seventy-six first class and 740 tourist class.
August 26, 1957: Left Gdynia on resumption of transatlantic service to Montreal.
December 28, 1965: Called at Boston, commencing occasional winter calls there.
December 1968: Withdrawn from transatlantic service.
April 1969: Withdrawn from service; sold to Municipality of Gdynia for use as a floating hotel; unsuccessful.
1971: Sold to Hong Kong shipbreakers.
May 11, 1971: Arrived at Hong Kong for scrapping.

Sobieski

Service: Post-war service 1946–50: Naples–Genoa–Cannes–Gibraltar–Halifax (westbound only)–New York.
Particulars: 11,030 gross tons; 511 × 67 × 26 feet.
Builders: Swan, Hunter & Wigham Richardson Ltd., Newcastle, England, 1939.
Machinery: B&W type diesels; twin screw; service speed 16 knots.
Capacity: Seventy first class, 270 cabin class, and 600 tourist class.

August 25, 1938: Launched.
May 1939: Maiden voyage: Gdynia–Rio de Janeiro–Buenos Aires; forty-four first class, 250 third class, and 860 steerage.
1940–45: Allied troopship.
1946–50: Genoa–New York service.
1950: Transferred to Sovtorgflot, U.S.S.R. flag; renamed *Gruzia*; used in Black Sea local service from Odessa; later occasional voyages Odessa–Havana.
April 14, 1975: Arrived at La Spezia in tow from Odessa to be scrapped.

In her gray hull coloring, the *Batory* calls at Tilbury. (*Alex Duncan collection*)

The former *Sobieski* is seen but in Soviet colors as the *Gruzia*. (*Mick Lindsay collection*)

The *Batory* in her black hull coloring. (*Author's collection*)

Stefan Batory

Service: Gdynia–Copenhagen–London or Southampton–Montreal; occasional calls at Rotterdam, Cuxhaven (Hamburg) and Quebec City. Winter cruising from London to the Canaries, West Africa, Mediterranean, Caribbean, etc.
Particulars: 15,043 gross tons; 503 × 69 × 28 feet.
Builders: Wilton-Fijenoord Shipyard, Schiedam, Holland, 1952.
Machinery: Steam turbines; single screw; service speed 16½ knots.
Capacity: Thirty-nine first class and 734 tourist class.

1952–68: Sailed as *Maasdam*, Holland-America Line, Dutch flag (qv).
September 1968: Transferred to Polish Ocean Lines, Polish flag; renamed *Stefan Batory*.
December 1968–March 1969: Major refit and modernization at Gdansk.
April 1969: First crossing as *Stefan Batory* to Montreal. First season: 93 percent load factor.
January 4, 1971: Arrived New York and met with anti-Communist protests; winter Caribbean cruise schedule unsuccessful.
April 11, 1970: Revisited Rotterdam; Holland-America Line acted as agents.
April 1972: Began calls at Hamburg.
January 1974: Eighty-one Polish crew jumped ship at Hamburg.
November 1974: 192 crew jumped ship.
1975: Discontinued calls at Copenhagen.
1976: Became one-class ship with 779 berths; calls at Quebec City discontinued.
1977: Mostly Gdynia–Rotterdam–Tilbury–Montreal service.
February 1979: Among other cruises, made fifty-two-day Mediterranean–Black Sea cruise.
1981: Because of political problems in Poland, many sailings terminated in Rotterdam instead of Gdynia.
December 1986: Rumored to be replaced by new, 20,000-grt *Polonia;* never materialized.
October 1987: Final transatlantic crossing.
March 1988: Last voyage for Polish Ocean Lines: West Indies–Cuba cruise departing from Tilbury. As *Stefan Batory* carried 180,259 passengers on 131 crossings and 86,049 on 136 cruises.
May 1988: Sold to Greek buyers (Hellenic Polish Line), Panamanian flag; renamed *Stefan*; intended refit for cruising never materialized.
June 1988: Laid-up at Flushing.
November 1988: Moved to Piraeus; further lay-up.
1989: Sold to Stena Line. Briefly used as film prop; renamed *Las Delicias*.
February 1, 1990: Arrived at Gothenburg; renamed *Stefan*; used as refugee accommodation ship. Later registered to Bahamian owners; laid-up in Perama Bay.
1991: Planned to be rebuilt as a cruise ship by Lelakis Group (Regency Cruises), but never materialized; remained laid-up.
March 24, 2000: Arrived at Aliağa, Turkey, to be scrapped.

The *Stefan Batory* at Gdynia. (*Author's collection*)

The last rites have begun at Aliağa in Turkey. (*Selim San collection*)

38

Shaw Savill Line

Southern Cross

Service: Occasional Southampton–Port Everglades sailings via Bermuda as part of full around-the-world sailings: Southampton–Bermuda–Port Everglades–Trinidad–Curaçao–Panama Canal–Tahiti–Fiji–Wellington–Auckland–Sydney–Melbourne–Fremantle–Durban–Cape Town–Las Palmas–Southampton.
Particulars: 20,204 gross tons; 604 × 78 × 26 feet.
Builders: Harland & Wolff Ltd., Belfast, Northern Ireland, 1955.
Machinery: Steam turbines; twin screw; service speed 20 knots.
Capacity: 1,100 all-tourist class.

August 17, 1954: Launched by HM Queen Elizabeth II.
March 29, 1955: Departed from Southampton on first around-the-world voyage; alternating eastabout and westabout.
1961: Commenced calls at Port Everglades.
1965: Given new funnel colors.
March 1971: Withdrawn from service; laid-up.
April 26, 1972: Moved to River Fal for further lay-up; offered for sale.
March 1973: Sold to Compañía de Vapores Cerula (Ulysses Line), Greek flag, for $1.8 million. Renamed *Calypso.*
March 18, 1973: Arrived at Piraeus for major refit.
June 20, 1975: Maiden cruise from Tilbury to Scandinavia.
1976: Cruises from New York.
December 1979: Operated jointly by Paquet Cruises and Ulysses Line for winter cruising to the Caribbean from Miami; summers to Alaska from Vancouver.
1980: Renamed *Calypso I.*
1981: Transferred to Western Cruise Lines, Panamanian flag; renamed *Azure Seas*; 821 one-class passengers.
1990: Transferred to Admiral Cruises, Liberian flag.
1992: Sold to Dolphin Cruise Lines, Bahamian registry; renamed *Ocean Breeze.*
1999: Sold to Imperial Majesty Cruise Lines.
April 2000: Began two-night cruises between Port Everglades and Nassau.
July 2003: Laid-up at Freeport.
October 5, 2003: Arrived at Chittagong for scrapping.

The innovative, engines-aft *Southern Cross* of 1955. (*Mick Lindsay collection*)

Special Occasion: The *Dominion Monarch* of 1939 (left) meets the *Southern Cross* at Wellington. (*Anton Logvinenko collection*)

39

Sitmar Line

Castel Felice

Service: Summers only: 1954–58 and during 1965: Bremerhaven–Le Havre–Southampton–New York or Quebec City; otherwise, Europe–Australia and around-the-world service.
Particulars: 12,478 gross tons; 493 × 64 × 25 feet.
Builders: Alexander Stephen & Sons Ltd., Glasgow, Scotland, 1930.
Machinery: Steam turbines; twin screw; service speed 17 knots.
Capacity: 1,405 all- tourist class passengers.

August 27, 1930: Launched as *Kenya* for British India Steam Navigation Co. Ltd., British flag.
December 1930: Entered Bombay–Durban service; 9,890 gross tons.
1940–46: British Government trooping.
1941: Renamed *Keren.*
April 1946: Sold to British Ministry of Transport; but laid-up.
1949: Renamed *Kenya*; then sold to Alva Steamship Co. (Sitmar Line), Panamanian flag.
1950: Renamed *Fairstone*; then reverted to *Kenya* and *Keren*; changed to Italian flag.
1951–52: Rebuilt at Antwerp and then completed at Genoa: 12,150 gross tons; renamed *Castel Felice.*
October 1952: Commenced migrant sailings to Australia and later to East Coast of South America.
1954: Transatlantic sailings from Bremerhaven, Le Havre, and Southampton to New York or Quebec City.
1955: Refitted at Genoa; tonnage relisted as 12,478.
1958: Further transatlantic crossings.
June 1965: Transatlantic crossings to New York for four months; proved uneconomical; resumed fulltime Australian service.
March 1969: Transferred from Sitmar Line, Italian flag to Passenger Line Service Inc., Panamanian flag; still operated by Sitmar Line and continued in Australian service; tonnage relisted as 10,952.
October 21, 1970: Arrived at Kaohsiung for scrapping.

The *Castel Felice* departs from Pier 45, New York in this 1965 photo. (*Mick Lindsay collection*)

Fairsea

Service: 1953 and 1957: Bremerhaven–Quebec City and Bremerhaven–New York sailings.
Particulars: 11,683 gross tons; 492 × 69 × 27 feet.
Builders: Sun Shipbuilding & Dry Dock Co., Chester, Pennsylvania, 1941.
Machinery: Doxford type diesel; single screw; service speed 16 knots.
Capacity: Forty first class and 1,400 tourist class.
Notes: Former auxiliary aircraft carrier.

March 1, 1941: Launched as *Rio de la Plata* for Moore-McCormack Lines, U.S. flag; combination passenger-cargo liner for New York–East Coast of South America service.
October 1941: Construction handed over to U.S. Navy; redesigned as auxiliary aircraft carrier; renamed *Charger.*
March 1942: Completed, but transferred to Royal Navy, British flag.
March 1946: Decommissioned; laid-up; declared surplus.
1949: Sold to Alvion Steamship Co. (Sitmar Line), Panamanian flag. Rebuilt at New York as a passenger ship; renamed *Fairsea*; tonnage listed as 11,883; 1,440 passengers.
1950: Entered Bremerhaven–Australia migrant service.
April 30, 1953: Commenced transatlantic service from Bremerhaven.
1957: Further transatlantic sailings.
1957–58: Rebuilt and modernized at Trieste; 13,432 gross tons; 1,460 all-tourist class passengers; transferred to Italian flag.
1958–69: Europe–Australia service: outward via Suez, homeward via Panama.
January 29, 1969: Serious engine room fire 900 miles west of Panama; drifted before being taken in tow by U.S. freighter *Louise Lykes*; brought to Balboa and laid-up.
August 6, 1969: Arrived in tow at La Spezia for scrapping.

Long and flat, the *Fairsea* takes a turn in dry dock at Southampton. (*Mick Lindsay collection*)

40

Spanish Line

Habana

Service: Spanish ports–Havana–New York.
Particulars: 10,069 gross tons; 500 × 61 × 28 feet.
Builders: Sociedad Española de Construcción Naval, Bilbao, Spain, 1923.
Machinery: Steam turbines; twin screw; service speed 16 knots.
Capacity: 112 first class passengers.

September 14, 1920: Launched as *Alfonso XIII* for Spanish Line, Spanish flag.
October 26, 1920: Seriously damaged in shipyard fire; completion delayed.
September 1923: Maiden voyage Spain–Havana–Vera Cruz; 1,100 passengers in three classes.
January 1927: Began sailings to New York.
1931: Renamed *Habana.*
1936–39: Laid-up at Bordeaux for safety during Spanish Civil War.
1939: Continued sailings to New York and to Gulf of Mexico ports.
1943: Seriously damaged by fire at Bilbao; rebuilt as twelve-passenger freighter.
1946–47: Rebuilt by Todd Shipyard at Brooklyn with 112 first class berths; later, Spain–Havana–New York service.
1953: Cargo sailings only; tonnage reduced to 8,279.
July 1960: Laid-up at Ferrol, Spain.
1963–64: Sold to Pescanova S/A, Spanish flag; renamed *Galicia*; converted to fish factory ship; tonnage relisted as 10,413.
1978: Scrapped in Spain.

Marques de Comillas

Service: Spanish ports–Havana–New York.
Particulars: 9,922 gross tons; 467 × 56 × 25 feet.
Builders: Sociedad Española de Construcción Naval, Ferrol, Spain, 1928.
Machinery: Steam turbines; twin screw; service speed 16 knots.
Capacity: 241 first class and 221 tourist class.

March 1927: Damaged during launching.
November 1928: Maiden voyage Cadiz–New York; 150 first class and 400 tourist class passengers.

Spain's long-lived *Habana*. (*Author's collection*)

Tropic Waters: The *Guadalupe* seen at San Juan, Puerto Rico. (*Frank Andrews collection*)

1936–39: Laid-up for safety during Spanish Civil War.
October 1939: Resumed Spain–Havana–New York sailings.
1953: Transferred to Spain–West Indies–Mexico service.
January 1961: Commenced major refit; accommodation restyled for 134 special tourist and 796 tourist class.
November 1961: Seriously damaged by fire at shipyard in Ferrol, Spain.
March 1962: Arrived at Bilbao for scrapping.

Covadonga

Service: Bilbao–Santander–Gijon–Vigo–Lisbon–New York–Havana or San Juan–Vera Cruz–New York–Coruna–Santander–Bilbao.
Particulars: 10,226 gross tons; 487 × 62 × 26 feet.
Builders: Compañía Euskalduna, Bilbao, Spain, 1953.
Machinery: Sulzer diesel; single screw; service speed 16½ knots.
Capacity: 105 first class and 248 tourist class.

1952: Launched as *Monasterio de la Rábida*, freighter for Compañía Empresa Nacional Elcano, Spanish flag; sold shortly after launching to Compañía Trasatlantica Espanola (Spanish Line), also Spanish flag; redesigned as a passenger ship; renamed *Covadonga*.
May 1953: Coronation cruise Spain-London.
August 27, 1953: Departed from Bilbao on maiden voyage to New York, etc.
July 1961: Made voyage Spain–Southampton.
1970–73: Variable scheduling including calls at New Orleans, Houston, Mobile, Miami, Norfolk, and Baltimore; also variable calls at Funchal, Tenerife, Cadiz, and Alicante. Passenger berthing reduced to seventy-five one-class and later to only twelve passengers.
January 19, 1973: Laid-up at Bilbao.
April 4, 1973: Arrived at Castellon for scrapping.

Guadalupe

Service: Bilbao–Santander–Gijon–Vigo–Lisbon–New York–Havana or San Juan–Vera Cruz–New York–Coruna–Santander-Bilbao.
Particulars: 10,226 gross tons; 487 × 62 × 26 feet.
Builders: Sociedad Española de Construcción Naval, Bilbao, Spain, 1953.
Machinery: Sulzer diesel; single screw; service speed 16½ knots.
Capacity: 105 first class and 244 tourist class.

1952: Launched as *Monasterio de Guadalupe*, freighter for Compañía Empresa Nacional Elcano, Spanish flag; sold shortly after launching to Compañía Trasatlantica Espanola (Spanish Line), also Spanish flag; redesigned as a passenger ship; renamed *Guadalupe.*
March 21, 1953: Departed from Bilbao on maiden voyage to New York, etc.
1970–73: Variable scheduling including calls at New Orleans, Houston, Mobile, Miami, Norfolk, and Baltimore; also variable calls at Funchal, Tenerife, Cadiz, and Alicante. Passenger berthing reduced to seventy-one one-class and later to only twelve passengers.
April 10, 1973: Arrived at Castellon for scrapping.

41

Splošna Plovba

Bothinj

Service: Rijeka–New York and other U.S. East Coast ports (Boston, Philadelphia, Baltimore, Charleston, etc.). Include various Mediterranean ports (Trieste, Genoa, Marseilles, Casablanca, etc.).
Particulars: 7,746 gross tons; 448 × 57 × 26 feet.
Builders: Cockerill S/A Shipyard, Hoboken, Belgium, 1941–46.
Machinery: B&W type diesel; single screw; service speed 14 knots.
Capacity: Fourteen first class and fifty-six tourist class.

1941: Under construction for Compagnie Maritime Belge (Belgian Line), Belgian flag; later launched by Nazi invasion forces.
1944: Scuttled in River Scheldt by retreating Nazis; later salvaged.
1946: Completed as *Gouverneur Galopin* for Compagnie Maritime Belge; Antwerp–East Coast of South America service.
1959: Sold to Splošna Plovba, Yugoslavian flag; renamed *Bothinj*; Rijeka–New York service.
January 12, 1972: Left Rijeka for Split for scrapping by Brodospas.

Bovec

Service: Rijeka–New York (see *Bothinj* for ports).
Particulars: 7,766 gross tons; 448 × 57 × 26 feet.
Builders: Cockerill S/A Shipyard, Hoboken, Belgium, 1941–45.
Machinery: B&W type diesel; single screw; service speed 14 knots.
Capacity: Fourteen first class and fifty-six tourist class.
1941: Under construction for Compagnie Maritime Belge (Belgian Line), Belgian flag; later launched by Nazi invasion forces.
1944: Scuttled in River Scheldt by retreating Nazis; later salvaged.
1946: Completed as *Armand Grisar* for Compagnie Maritime Belge; Antwerp–East Coast of South America service.
1959: Sold to Splošna Plovba, Yugoslavian flag; renamed *Bothinj*; Rijeka–New York service.
December 1970: Sold to Chinese shipbreakers and scrapped at Whampoa.

Bled

Service: Rijeka–New York & other U.S. East Coast ports (see *Bothinj*).
Particulars: 7,761 gross tons; 448 × 57 × 26 feet.
Builders: Cockerill S/A Shipyard, Hoboken, Belgium, 1942–45.
Machinery: B&W type diesel; single screw; service speed 14 knots.
Capacity: Sixty tourist class.

1942: Intended for Compagnie Maritime Belge, Belgian flag, but launched as Nazi-German freighter *Kanomier.*
May 1945: Found in the Baltic; later returned to the Belgians.
1946: Rebuilt for Compagnie Maritime Belge as *Alex van Opstal*; later Antwerp–East Coast of South America service.
1959: Sold to Splošna Plovba, Yugoslavian flag; renamed *Bled*; Rijeka–New York service.
1970: Scrapped at La Spezia.

42

Sven Salén/Salén Line

Anna Salén

Service: 1949–55: Periodic Bremerhaven–New York/Halifax/Quebec City voyages; occasionally including other North European ports.
Particulars: 11,672 gross tons; 492 × 69 × 28 feet.
Builders: Sun Shipbuilding & Dry Dock Co., Chester, Pennsylvania, 1940.
Machinery: Busch-Sulzer diesel; single screw; service speed 17 knots.
Capacity: Approximately 1,000 one-class passengers (sometimes listed as high as 1,500 berths).

August 1, 1939: Laid down as freighter *Mormacland* for Moore-McCormack Lines, U.S. flag.
December 14, 1939: Launched.
April 1940: Completed.
March 1941: Transferred to U.S. Navy and converted by Atlantic Iron Works, Brooklyn to an escort aircraft carrier; then assigned to Lend Lease Program and transferred to Great Britain.
November 1941: Commissioned for Royal Navy as *HMS Archer*; sister ship to *USS Long Island* (later *Seven Seas* (qv)); crew of 555.
January 13, 1942: Serious collision with Peruvian steamer *Brazos* in western Atlantic; *Archer* had to be towed stern-first to Charleston Naval Shipyard.
February 20, 1943: Inspected by King George VI at Liverpool.
November 1943: Serious mechanical troubles; eventually used as a stores ship in the Gareloch.
March 1944: Towed to Loch Alsh; used as an accommodation ship.

Austere Quarters: The migrant ship *Anna Salén*. (*Author's collection*)

August 1944: Towed to Belfast for extensive repairs which took seven and a half months.
March 1945: Transferred to the Ministry of War Transport; renamed *Empire Lagan*; freighter service under management of Blue Funnel Line.
January 1946: Returned to U.S. Navy; laid-up at Norfolk.
September 1947: Sold to American buyers for freighter service but never materialized.
1948: Sold to Sven Salén, Swedish flag; renamed *Anna Salén*; rebuilt as a bulk carrier at Bethlehem Steel Shipyard, Baltimore; made one voyage with coal to Italy. Change in plans and ship converted for passenger service in Italy.
May 1949: First passenger voyage: Naples–Suez–Melbourne–Sydney with migrants.
December 1949: Broke down in Indian Ocean; limped to Aden; passengers transferred to *Skaugum* (qv).
1949–55: Varied migrant voyages as well as several trooping voyages between Marseilles and Saigon for the French Government.
June 1952: Used as a ferry between Stockholm and Helsinki for Olympic Games at Helsinki.
August 13, 1952: Collision with Norwegian whaler *Thorshøvdi* in the Pentland Firth.
1955: Sold to Compagnia Navigazione Tasmania S/A, Greek flag; renamed *Tasmania*; used on Mediterranean–Australia migrant service under management of Hellenic Mediterranean Lines, Greek flag.
1958: Converted to freighter; tonnage reduced to 7,638.
1961: Sold to China Union Lines, Taipei flag; renamed *Union Reliance*; Far East–U.S. freighter service.
November 7, 1961: Collided with Norwegian tanker *Berea* in the Houston Ship Channel; *Union Reliance* caught fire and was abandoned. Wreck later towed by U.S. Coast Guard to Galveston. Ship and her cargo seized by U.S. authorities for debts.
January 1962: Sold to New Orleans scrappers for $109,000.
March 1962: Scrapped.

43

Swedish American Line

Gripsholm (1925)

Service: Gothenburg–Copenhagen–New York service; sometimes via Bremerhaven and Halifax (westbound only).
Particulars: 19,105 gross tons; 590 × 74 × 29 feet.
Builders: Sir W G Armstrong-Whitworth & Co., Newcastle, England, 1925.
Machinery: B&W type diesels; twin screw; service speed 16½ knots.
Capacity: 210 first class and 710 tourist class.
Notes: First transatlantic liner to be driven by diesels.

November 26, 1924: Launched.
November 21, 1925 Nov: Departed from Gothenburg on maiden voyage to New York; 17,993 gross tons; 127 first class, 482 second class, and 948 third class. Considerable cruising.
1932: Repainted with white hull.
1937: Major refit: tonnage relisted as 18,134.
1940–46: Used as International Red Cross exchange ship for diplomats, refugees, prisoners, etc.
March 1946: Resumed Gothenburg–New York sailings.
1949–50: Major refit at Kiel; new funnels fitted; given new bow and lengthened from 573 to 590 feet; tonnage relisted as 19,105; accommodation modernized and restyled for 210 first class and 910 tourist class.
December 29, 1953: Final sailing Gothenburg–New York.
February 1, 1954: Began sailing as *Gripsholm* but for Bremen-America Line (partnership of Swedish American Line and North German Lloyd); later renamed *Berlin* (qv).

Sailing for the Bremen-America Line, the *Gripsholm* has been repainted with North German Lloyd funnel colors. (*ALF collection*)

Stockholm

Service: Gothenburg–Copenhagen–New York; sometimes westbound calls at Bremerhaven and Halifax. Occasional cruising.
Particulars: 11,700 gross tons; 525 × 69 × 24 feet.
Builders: A/B Götaverken Shipyard, Gothenburg, Sweden, 1948.
Machinery: Götaverken diesels; twin screw; service speed 19 knots.
Capacity: 113 first class and 282 tourist class.
Notes: Became world's first trade union holiday ship.

September 9, 1946: Launched; first transatlantic passenger ship to be launched following World War II; the largest passenger ship yet built in Sweden.
February 21, 1948: Departed from Gothenburg on maiden voyage to New York.
1952: Major refit: Accommodation enlarged for eighty-six first class and 584 tourist class; tonnage relisted as 12,644.
1955: First class accommodation reduced to 24 berths.
February 1956: Rumored to be transferring to newly formed Denmark-America Line for Copenhagen–New York service; never materialized.
July 25–26, 1956: Rammed and sank Italian liner *Andrea Doria* in fog off Nantucket; fifty-two casualties.

Above: Outbound in New York's Upper Bay, the *Stockholm* has endured for nearly seventy years. (*ALF collection*)

Left: Idle at Southampton in 1985. (*Author's collection*)

July–December 1956: Repairs including new bow at Bethlehem Steel Shipyard, Brooklyn.
December 8, 1956: Resumed sailing.
January 3, 1960: Sold and delivered to Deutsche Seereederei, East German flag; renamed *Völkerfreundschaft;* refitted for 568 one-class passengers; tonnage relisted as 12,387. World's first trade union holiday ship: workers' cruises from Rostock (to U.S.S.R., Black Sea, Egypt, Cuba, etc.). Later occasional summer charters to Stena Line, Swedish flag, for Scandinavian cruises.
August 1960: Grounded at Sandhamn.
1972: Tonnage relisted as 12,068.
April 1985: Sold to Neptunus Rex Enterprises, Panamanian flag; renamed *Volker.*
August 1985: Laid-up in the Oslofjord.
December 1985: Moved to Southampton; laid-up; offered for sale.
December 20, 1986: Sailed Southampton–Oslo for use as a refugee accommodation ship; renamed *Fridjof Nansen.*
May 1989: Sold to StarLauro Cruises, Italian flag; ship moved to Genoa and to be rebuilt as cruise ship *Surriento*, then *Positano*; plans never materialized.
1990: Sold to Genoa dock owner Vittorio Chiesa.
1992–93: Extensively rebuilt as a modern cruise ship at Genoa; renamed *Italia I* for Nina Cruise Lines, Italian flag; 566 passengers.
1994: Renamed *Italia Prima.*
1998: Used as hotel ship at Expo 98 at Lisbon.
September 1998: Chartered Valtur Tourist Co. and renamed *Valtur Prima.* Later Caribbean cruises including calls in Cuba.
July 2002: Sold to Festival Cruises; renamed *Caribe.*
January 2005: Sold to Classic International Cruises, Madeira flag; renamed *Athena.* Worldwide charter cruising.
September 15, 2012: Arrested at Marseilles following collapse of Classic International Cruises.

February 2013: Sold to Portuscale Cruises, Madeira flag; later renamed *Azores*. Continued in charter cruise service.
2016–17: Renamed *Astoria* and chartered to Rivages du Monde.
April 2017: Reported to remain in service until December 2018.
2018: Reached seventieth year.
2019: Charter cruising, including the west coast of Mexico.

Kungsholm (1953)

Service: Gothenburg–Copenhagen–New York (occasional westbound calls at Bremerhaven and Halifax); also considerable cruising from New York.
Particulars: 21,141 gross tons; 600 × 77 × 26 feet.
Builders: De Schelde Shipyard, Flushing, Holland, 1953.
Machinery: B&W type diesels; twin screw; service speed 19 knots.
Capacity: 176 first class and 626 tourist class; 425 one-class for cruising.

April 18, 1952: Launched by HRH Princess Sibylla of Sweden.
November 24, 1953: Left Gothenburg on maiden voyage to New York.
November 1961: Refit.
October 16, 1965: Sold to North German Lloyd, West German flag; renamed *Europa* (qv).

The handsome *Kungsholm* makes a late afternoon arrival off Lower Manhattan. (*ALF collection*)

Above left: Greatly rebuilt, the *Azores* (ex-*Stockholm*) seen departing from Reykjavik during a summer cruise in 2015. (*Author's collection*)

Above right: The grand launching of the *Kungsholm*. (*ALF collection*)

Like a big yacht, the *Gripsholm* was one of the most beautiful liners of the 1950s. (*Anton Logvinenko collection*)

As the renamed *Sea*, the ex-*Gripsholm* idle at Tampa in her final days. (*Peter Knego collection*)

Gripsholm (1957)

Service: Gothenburg–Copenhagen–New York (occasional westbound calls at Bremerhaven and Halifax); also considerable cruising from New York.
Particulars: 23,191 gross tons; 631 × 82 × 27 feet.
Builders: Ansaldo Shipyard, Genoa, Italy, 1957.
Machinery: Götaverken type diesels; twin screw; service speed 19 knots.
Capacity: 214 first class and 628 tourist class; 450 one-class for cruising.

May 10, 1955: Laid down.
April 8, 1956: Launched by HRH Princess Margaretha of Sweden.
May 14, 1957: Left Gothenburg on maiden voyage to New York.
October 1974: Plans abandoned to transfer ship to Panamanian flag.
August 26, 1975: Withdrawn and laid-up; offered for sale.
October 1975: Rumored to be sold to Chandris Lines, Greek flag, but failed to materialize.
December 19, 1975: Sold to Karageorgis Cruises (Nautilus Armadora S/A), Greek flag; renamed *Navarino*; refitted for Mediterranean, South American and South African cruising.
August 8, 1981: Aground off Patmos; badly damaged.
October 1981: Sold to Sally Line, West German flag; intended for use with Commodore Cruises; Miami–Caribbean service.
October 29, 1981: Accommodation damaged by fire during short Piraeus–Skaramangas voyage.
November 26, 1981: Floating dry dock collapsed causing severe damages to *Navarino;* thought to be a complete loss; later endured complicated salvage by British–Greek–Swedish consortium.
May 1982: Ship fully refloated; Sally Line withdrew from final purchase; ship sold to Greek buyers for use as moored accommodation ship; never materialized.
June 1983: Sold to Multi Ship Italia, Italian flag; renamed *Samantha*; intended to become condo-style cruise ship; never materialized.
August 1984: Sold to Lelakis Group, Greek flag.
October 13, 1984: Arrived under tow at Piraeus for full repairs; renamed *Regent Sea.*
November 1985: Began operations for Regency Cruises.
1987: Panamanian flag.
1990: Bahamian flag.
1995: Seized for debt following collapse of Regency Cruises.
1997: Laid-up at Freeport and later Tampa. Reportedly sold to owners identified as New York Cruise Line and renamed *Sea*; then to become casino ship *Splash*; neither role materialized. Ship remained *Sea.*
1998–99: Rumored to be bought by Swedish investors with plans to make her a hotel at Stockholm.
July 12, 2001: Sank off South Africa while empty and under tow on voyage from Tampa to Alang, India.

Kungsholm (1966)

Service: Gothenburg–Copenhagen–New York, but mostly cruising from New York.
Particulars: 26,678 gross tons; 660 × 86 × 26 feet.
Builders: John Brown & Co. Ltd., Clydebank, Scotland, 1966.
Machinery: Götaverken type diesels; twin screw; service speed 21 knots.
Capacity: 108 first class and 642 tourist class; 425 one-class for cruising.

The *Kungsholm* in Flagship Cruises' colors. (*ALF collection*)

The former *Kungsholm* as the rebuilt *Sea Princess*, berthed at Lisbon. (*Luis Miguel Correia*)

April 14, 1965: Launched.
March 11, 1966: Transferred to dry dock at Belfast; completion delayed by three months.
May 2, 1966: Arrived in New York on maiden voyage from Gothenburg.
October 1974: Plans shelved for transfer to Panamanian flag.
December 1975: Withdrawn and laid-up, thereby ending Swedish American Line passenger service; later sold to Flagship Cruises (Øivind Lorentzen), Liberian flag; retained original name; cruising only.
January 14, 1978: Refloating began in Fort de France Bay after going aground; completely refloated on January 19.
September 1978 Sep: Sold to P&O Cruises (Sea Leasing Corp), British flag; renamed *Sea Princess*; major refit at Bremerhaven; forward funnel removed.
January 20, 1979: Departed from Hong Kong for Sydney for Pacific cruising.
1982: Major refit at Southampton; additional accommodation added; capacity relisted as 840.
1984: Capacity relisted as 720.
April 1995: Renamed *Victoria*.
December 1999: Charter to make Around Africa cruise to celebrate Union-Castle Line; funnel repainted in Union-Castle colors.
December 2002: Sold to Leonardo Shipping Co., Bahamian flag; renamed *Mona Lisa*; used for charter cruising.
December 2006: Used as hotel ship for Asian Games at Doha.
2007: Renamed *Oceanic II* for charter to Pullmanturs.
April 2008: Reverted to *Mona Lisa*; charter to Lord Nelson Cruises.
2009: Peace Boat charter.
February 2010: Used as accommodation ship during Winter Olympics at Vancouver.
2010: Final season with Lord Nelson Cruises.
September 2010: Laid-up; then sold to Daewoo Shipbuilding Co.; sailed to Duqm, Oman, and converted to floating hotel.
December 2011: Renamed *Veronica*; opened as hotel.
October 2013: Hotel operation closed down; ship idle at Duqm. Rumor that Swedish investors would buy ship for use as a moored cruise terminal in Stockholm harbor; never materialized.
November 19, 2015: Arrived at Alang for demolition.

44

Turkish Maritime Lines

Tarsus

Service: Periodic Istanbul–New York sailings; otherwise inter-Mediterranean service and cruising.
Particulars: 9,451 gross tons; 475 × 62 × 27 feet.
Builders: New York Shipbuilding Co., Camden, New Jersey, 1931.
Machinery: Steam turbines; single screw; service speed 16 knots.
Capacity: 189 first class, sixty-six second class, and 210 third class.

1930: Launched as *Exochorda* for American Export Lines, U.S. flag.
1931: Entered New York–Mediterranean service; 9,360 gross tons; 125 all-first class passengers.
October 1940: Acquired by U.S. Navy; renamed *Harry Lee.*
1941–46: Wartime transport service.
1946: Declared surplus; sold to Turkish Maritime Lines, Turkish flag; renamed *Tarsus.* Major refit at Baltimore; tonnage relisted as 9,451; accommodation restyled as 189 first class, sixty-six second class, and 210 third class.
June 1960: Chartered to Fiesta Cruise Lines for summer season of weekly New York–Bermuda cruises.
December 1960: Destroyed by fire in the Bosporus after being rammed by blazing ship following collision of tankers *Peter Zoranic* and *World Harmony.*

45

United Arab Maritime Co.

Star of Assuan

Service: April–December: Alexandria–Naples–Genoa–Montreal–Hamilton. Ports often varied.
Particulars: 5,464 gross tons; 398 × 55 × 23 feet.
Builders: Caledon Shipbuilding & Engineering Co. Ltd., Greenock, Scotland, 1948.
Machinery: Doxford diesel; single screw; service speed 14 knots.
Capacity: Forty all-tourist class.

June 21, 1948: Launched for Alexandria Navigation Co. Ltd., Egyptian flag; freighter with twelve passenger berths; later extended to forty berths.
June 1959: Began Great Lakes service.
December 1959: Transferred to Société Générale pour la Navigation Co., Egyptian flag.
July 1961: Transferred to Khedivial Mail Line, Egyptian flag; soon transferred to United Arab Maritime Co., Egyptian flag. Operation also known as Canada-Orient Line.
1963–64: Transferred to Alexandria–Mediterranean–Baltic service.
1983: Scrapped at Alexandria.

Star of Suez

Service: Same as *Star of Assuan*.
Particulars: 6,440 gross tons; 408 × 56 × 23 feet.
Builders: Cantieri Riuniti dell'Adriatico, Trieste, Italy, 1948.
Machinery: Sulzer diesel; single screw; service speed 14 knots.
Capacity: Forty tourist class.

August 2, 1948: Launched for Alexandria Navigation Co. Ltd., Egyptian flag; freighter with twelve passenger berths; later extended to forty passengers.

The Egyptian combo ship *Star of Assuan*. (*Gillespie-Faber collection*)

The *Cleopatra* in United Arab Maritime Co. colors. (*Author's collection*)

June 1959: Began Mediterranean–Great Lakes service.
1961: Transferred to Société Générale pour la Navigation Maritime, Egyptian flag; soon transferred to United Arab Maritime Co., Egyptian flag; also known as Canada-Orient Line.
1963–65: Alexandria–Lisbon–Montreal–Hamilton service; afterward downgraded to freighter service including Alexandria–Mediterranean–Baltic.
1977: Laid-up at Alexandria.
1983: Scrapped at Alexandria.

Salah El Din

Service: Seasonal service: Alexandria–Marseilles–Naples–Leghorn–Genoa–Lisbon–Montreal–Toledo–Hamilton (Ontario).
Particulars: 8,199 gross tons; 455 × 62 × 28 feet.
Builders: California Shipbuilding Corp., Los Angeles, California, 1944.
Machinery: Steam turbines; single screw; service speed 15 knots.
Capacity: 100 all-first class passengers.

1948–60: Sailed as *Mohammed Ali El Kebir*, Khedivial Mail Line, Egyptian flag (qv).
1960: Renamed *Salah El Din*.
1961–63: Periodic sailings between Mediterranean and Canada and Great Lakes ports.
September 4, 1963: Damaged by fire at Hamilton, Ontario; later sold to Liberian-flag buyers and renamed *Mercantile Victory*.
1965: Scrapped at Castellon, Spain.

Cleopatra

Service: Seasonal service: Alexandria–Marseilles–Naples–Leghorn–Genoa–Lisbon–Montreal–Toledo–Hamilton (Ontario).
Particulars: 8,193 gross tons; 455 × 62 × 28 feet.
Builders: Oregon Shipbuilding Corp., Portland, Oregon, 1944.
Machinery: Steam turbines; single screw; service speed 15 knots.
Capacity: 100 all-first class passengers.
Notes: First Victory Ship built in America.

1948–56: Sailed as *Khedive Ismail* for Khedivial Mail Line, Egyptian flag (qv).
1956–62: Sailed *Cleopatra* for Khedivial Mail Line.
1962: Transferred to United Arab Maritime Co., Egyptian flag.
May 1963–November 1965: Transatlantic service to Eastern Canada.
February 1966: Rammed quayside at Adabiya, Egypt; badly damaged. Later repaired and resumed sailing as a freighter.
November 13, 1975: Boiler explosion off Hartlepool, England; one crewmember killed. Later repaired.
March 1976: Returned to Alexandria; later scrapped.

46

United States Lines

Washington

Service: Post-war 1948–51: Austerity service New York–Cobh–Le Havre–Southampton (sometimes. to Bremerhaven as well).
Particulars: 29,627 gross tons; 705 × 86 feet.
Builders: New York Shipbuilding Co., Camden, New Jersey, 1933.
Machinery: Steam turbines; twin screw; service speed 20 knots.
Capacity: 1,106 in single, low-fare class.

August 20, 1932: Launched.
May 10, 1933: Maiden voyage: New York–Le Havre–Southampton–Hamburg; 24,289 gross tons; 580 cabin class, 400 tourist class, and 150 third class.
1940–41: Cruising from New York owing to war in Europe.
June 1941: Transferred to U.S. Navy; renamed *Mount Vernon*; converted to troopship.
September 1942: Sold to U.S. Government.
1945: Reverted to name *Washington.*
January 1946: Transferred to U.S. Maritime Commission.
February 1948: Resumed New York–Southampton service under charter to United States Lines.
October 12, 1951: Withdrawn from transatlantic service.
1952: Laid-up in Hudson River Reserve Fleet at Jones Point, New York; later transferred to U.S. Dept. of Commerce.
June 30, 1964: Sold to Union Minerals & Alloys Corp. for $238,126.
June 28, 1965: Arrived in tow at Kearny, New Jersey, for scrapping.

America

Service: New York–Cobh–Le Havre–Southampton–Bremerhaven.
Particulars: 33,532 gross tons; 723 × 93 × 29 feet.
Builders: Newport News Shipbuilding & Dry Dock Co., Newport News, Virginia, 1940.
Machinery: Steam turbines; twin screw; service speed 22 knots.
Capacity: 516 first class, 371 cabin class, and 159 tourist class; 425 one-class.
Notes: Flagship of U.S. merchant marine 1940–52.

October 21, 1937: Ordered.
August 22, 1938: Keel laid.

The *Washington* in her post-war guise. (*Author's collection*)

The *America* on a snowy winter's day at the Columbus Quay, Bremerhaven. (*Mick Lindsay collection*)

August 31, 1939: Launched by Mrs. Franklin D. Roosevelt.
July 1940: Completed; tonnage listed as 26,424; original squat funnels soon had to be raised.
August 1940: Began cruising from New York owing to war in Europe.
1941–46: Transferred to U.S. Navy; refitted as troopship.
1942: Renamed *USS West Point*.
July 22, 1946: Decommissioned from military service; reverted to *America*; major refit followed.
November 14, 1946: First post-war sailing from New York to Southampton.
November 1949: Tonnage relisted as 33,532.
December 1960: Refit: Accommodation restyled as 516 first class and 530 tourist class.
September 1963: Began six-month lay-up at Todd Shipyard, Hoboken, following onboard labor dispute; resumed sailing February 1964.
August 28, 1964: Sold to Chandris Lines (Okeania S/A), Greek flag, for nearly $4 million.
November 1964: Delivered to Chandris at Newport News Shipyard; renamed *Australis* (qv).

United States

Service: New York–Le Havre–Southampton–Bremerhaven; off-season cruising in later years.
Particulars: 53,329 gross tons; 990 × 101 × 28 feet.
Builders: Newport News Shipbuilding & Dry Dock Co., Newport News, Virginia, 1952.
Machinery: Steam turbines; twin screw; service speed 30 knots.
Capacity: 871 first class, 508 cabin class, and 551 tourist class.
Notes: World's fastest passenger liner; flagship of U.S. merchant marine.

February 8, 1950: Laid-down.
June 23, 1951: Floated in graving dock (not launched).
June 1952: Completely highly successful sea trials, reaching as much as 43 knots; total cost $77 million.
July 3, 1952: Left New York on maiden crossing; captured Blue Riband from *Queen Mary*; average speed 35.39 knots.
January 23, 1969: Began longest sailing of her career: thirty-nine days to South America and Africa; 19,000 miles.
May 1, 1969: First call at Boston as part of eastbound crossing.
November 8, 1969: Arrived at Newport News Shipyard; laid-up indefinitely, later at Norfolk.
April 1973: Sold to U.S. Federal Government for $4.6 million; continued in lay-up.
November 1978: Reportedly sold to United States Cruises Inc. for $5 million.
September 1979: Proposed use as a cruise ship between California and Hawaii (and on some longer cruises); projected condominium-style accommodation; later planned for 1,700 one-class passengers. Reactivation project sluggish and problematic.
May 1980: Dry docked at Norfolk for first time in over eleven years; then returned to lay-up.
August 1980: Reported to be under consideration by U.S. Navy for conversion into hospital ship and especially for Middle Eastern deployment.
1983: Bids submitted to rebuild the ship for cruising; Germany yards at Hamburg seemed most promising; never materialized.

1984: Rebuilding contract signed with HDW Shipyard at Hamburg, but then canceled.
April 27, 1992: Auctioned off debt to Marmara Marine Inc.
June 4, 1992: Departed from Newport News under tow for Istanbul and later mooring at Tuzla.
1993: Changed to Panama registry. Amidst many rumors of revival, proposal to operate ship under Cunard management and in tandem with the *Queen Elizabeth 2*. The Cunard ship would operate from New York; the *United States* from Port Everglades.
November 1, 1993: Towed to Sevastopol for removal of asbestos.
May 15, 1994: Returned to Tuzla; laid-up.
July 1996: Towed from Tuzla to Philadelphia (Boston, Baltimore, and New York had been considered); further lay-up.
November 1996: Auctioned-off to businessman Edward Cantor. Further rumor of restoration as a cruise ship.
April 2003: Rumored to be refitted and restored by Norwegian Cruise Lines for U.S.-flag cruise operations; never materialized.
2010: Plan to make ship over as a moored entertainment center and casino at or near Philadelphia.
2015: Reported studies made about scrapping the ship at either Bordentown, New Jersey; at Chester, Pennsylvania; or at Brownsville, Texas.
2016: Crystal Cruises considered restoring the ship for a reported $400–500 million; plan later dropped. Also rumored to become a floating power station moored along Brooklyn waterfront.
2018: Studies underway to use the ship as an entertainment center moored at Pier 57, New York.

Commencing her Record-Breaking Maiden Voyage: The *United States* departs on July 3, 1952. (*Author's collection*)

Sparkling: Overnight at Bremerhaven. (*ALF collection*)

Winter's Morning at New York in 1962. *From top to bottom*: the *Atlantic*, the *United States*, the *France*, and the *Queen Mary*. (*Port Authority of New York & New Jersey*)

Being moved for dry dock inspection in 1980. (*Norshipco*)

Laid-up at Philadelphia. (*Andy Kilk collection*)

47

Zim Lines

Jerusalem (1913)

Service: Genoa–Piraeus–Malta–Naples–Gibraltar–Halifax (westbound only)–New York.
Particulars: 11,015 gross tons; 530 × 61 feet.
Builders: Cammell Laird & Co. Ltd., Birkenhead, England, 1913.
Machinery: Steam turbines; twin screw; service speed 15 knots.
Capacity: Thirty-two first class and 741 tourist class.
Notes: First Atlantic liner in Israeli merchant marine.

1913–46: Sailed as *Bergensfjord,* Norwegian America Line, Norwegian flag.
1946–53: Sailed as *Argentina,* Home Lines, Panamanian flag (qv).
February 1953: Purchased by Zim Lines, Israeli flag; renamed *Jerusalem.*
April 29, 1953: Departed from Haifa on first sailing to New York.
1955: Permanently assigned to Haifa–Marseilles service.
1957: Renamed *Aliya.*
1958: Laid-up; considered for use as a hotel for World's Fair at Brussels; never materialized.
August 13, 1959: Arrived at La Spezia for scrapping.

The veteran *Jerusalem* at New York's Pier 42 in 1953. (*Cronican-Arroyo collection*)

Israel

Service: Haifa–Piraeus–Naples–Palma–Gibraltar–Halifax–New York; ports sometimes varied.
Particulars: 9,853 gross tons; 501 × 65 × 27 feet.
Builders: Deutsche Werft A/G, Hamburg, West Germany, 1955.
Machinery: Steam turbines; single screw; service speed 18 knots.
Capacity: Twenty-four first class, 232 tourist class, and fifty-six interchangeable.
Notes: First newly built passenger ship fort Israeli owners.

March 4, 1955: Launched; paid for as part of West German reparations to Israel.
September 4, 1955: Maiden voyage Hamburg–Southampton–Haifa.
October 13, 1955: Departed Haifa on maiden voyage to New York.
October 29, 1959: Rammed by freighter *American Press,* United States Lines, in New York harbor; one crewman killed; towed to Todd Shipyard, Brooklyn, for repairs.
March 25, 1966: Withdrawn from Zim passenger service; later sold to Empresa Insulana, Portuguese flag; renamed *Angra Do Heroísmo*; Lisbon–Madeira–Azores service.
1974: Scrapped at Castellon, Spain.

The *Zion* is being docked at Pier 64, New York, in 1962. (*Port Authority of New York & New Jersey*)

Seen at Miami: The greatly rebuilt former *Zion* as the cruise ship *Dolphin*. (*Luis Miguel Correia*)

Zion

Service: Haifa–Piraeus–Naples–Palma–Gibraltar–Halifax–New York; ports sometimes varied.
Particulars: 9,855 gross tons; 501 × 65 × 27 feet.
Builders: Deutsche Werft A/G, Hamburg, West Germany, 1956.
Machinery: Steam turbines; single screw; service speed 18 knots.
Capacity: Twenty-four first class, 232 tourist class, and fifty-six interchangeable.

July 19, 1955: Launched; reparations from West Germany to Israel.
February 19, 1956: Maiden voyage: Hamburg–Le Havre–Southampton–Messina–Haifa.
1956 9 Mar: Departed from Haifa on maiden voyage to New York.
1966 14 Apr: Withdrawn from Zim passenger service; later sold to Sociedade Geral de Comercio, Industria e Transportes, Portuguese flag; sale price $2.3 million; renamed *Amelia De Mello*; Lisbon–Canary Islands–Azores service; tonnage relisted as 10,195.
August 1971: Laid-up at Lisbon; offered for sale.
1972: Sold to Ulysses Line (Compañía de Vapores Realma S/A), Greek flag; renamed *Ithaca*.
May 9, 1972: Arrived at Bilbao for rebuilding as cruise ship; 760 one-class passengers; tonnage relisted as 8,977; Mediterranean cruising.
1978: Renamed *Dolphin IV* under operation of Ulysses Line, Panamanian flag.
January 1979: Began Miami–Nassau cruises.
1990: Transferred to Ulysses Cruises, but under operation of Dolphin Cruises: short cruises between Miami and the Bahamas.
October 2000: Laid-up at Freeport.
February 11, 2003: Departed Freeport under tow for Alang.
April 12, 2003: Arrived at Alang to be scrapped.

Jerusalem (1957)

Service: Periodic crossings: Haifa–Limassol–Piraeus–Naples–Gibraltar–Halifax–New York; ports sometimes varied; otherwise, Haifa–Marseilles service. Winter cruising from New York to the Caribbean.
Particulars: 9,920 gross tons; 487 × 65 × 21 feet.
Builders: Deutsche Werft A/G, Hamburg, West Germany, 1957.
Machinery: Steam turbines; twin screw; service speed 18 knots.
Capacity: 102 first class and 471 tourist class.

1958: Built as part of West German reparations to Israel; commissioned for Haifa–Marseilles service; also occasional crossings and winter crossing from New York.
1964: Converted for extended cruise service by Ocean Shipyard, Haifa.
1966: Commenced three-year charter to Peninsular & Occidental Steamship Co. for Miami–Bahamas cruise service; renamed *Miami.*
1968: Charter canceled; sold to Eastern Steamship Lines, Liberian flag; renamed *New Bahama Star*; $5 million refit at Jacksonville; original steam whistle transferred from predecessor *Bahama Star* (ex-*Arosa Star*, qv).
March 10, 1969: Maiden voyage from Miami to Nassau.
October 31, 1969: Grounded off Miami; later refloated.
1972: Renamed *Bahama Star;* transferred to Bahamas Shipping Corp., Liberian flag, but continued in Eastern Steamship Lines service.
October 27, 1974: Boiler damages.
1975: Sold to Venezolana de Cruceros del Caribe, Venezuelan flag; renamed *Bonaire Star*; intended for Caribbean cruise service from La Guaira, but laid-up at Mobile.
April 1979: Sold to Southern Metals Co. for $322,000.
May 8, 1979: Left Mobile under tow for New Orleans to be scrapped.
May 1979: Resold to West German buyers; then resold to Taiwanese scrappers at Kaohsiung.
October 3, 1979: Sank in the Pacific while empty and tow by tug *Jantar.*

Shalom

Service: Haifa–Naples–Marseilles–Malaga–New York; occasionally other Mediterranean ports. Winter cruising.
Particulars: 25,320 gross tons; 629 × 82 × 26 feet.
Builders: Chantiers de l'Atlantique, Saint-Nazaire, France, 1964.
Machinery: Steam turbines; twin screw; service speed 20 knots.
Capacity: Seventy-two first class and 1,018 tourist class; 650 one-class for cruises.
November 10, 1962: Launched by Mrs. David Ben-Gurion; cost $25 million and paid for by West German reparations to Israel; original intention was name ship *King Solomon*, then *King David.*
April 17, 1964: Left Haifa on maiden voyage to New York.
November 26, 1964: Rammed Norwegian tanker *Stolt Dagali* near Ambrose Light, New York; stern section of the tanker later sank; nineteen casualties. *Shalom* had $575,000 worth of damages; repaired at Todd Shipyard, Brooklyn.
1967: Sold to German-Atlantic Line, West German flag, for some $14 million.
November 1967: Transferred; renamed *Hanseatic* (qv).

Joyous Welcome: The *Shalom* arrives at New York on her maiden voyage. (*ALF collection*)

Bibliography

Bonsor, N. R. P., North Atlantic Seaway, Vols. 4–5 (Jersey, Channel Islands: Brookside Publications, 1978–79)

Cooke, A., *Liners & Cruise Ships-2* (London: Carmania Press Ltd., 2000)

De Boer, G. J., *125 Years: Holland-America Line* (Alkmaar, Holland: De Alk Publishing, 1998)

Fiebig, R., Heine, F., and Lose, F., *Great Passenger Ships of the World* (Hamburg: Koehlers Publishing Co., 2015)

Haws, D., *Merchant Fleets: Holland-America Line* (Uckfield, England: TCL Publications, 1995)

Heine, F., and Lose, F., *Great Passenger Ships of the World* (Hamburg: Koehlers Publishing Co., 2010)

Kludas, A., *Great Passenger Ships of the World* (Vols. 1–5); *Great Passenger Ships of the World* (Wellingborough, Northamptonshire: Patrick Stephens Ltd., 1984, 1992); *Great Passenger Ships of the World* (Hamburg: Koehlers Publishing Co., 1987, 1997)

Kludas, A., Heine, F., and Lose, F., *The Great Passenger Ships of the World* (Hamburg: Koehlers Publishing Co., 2002, 2006)

Miller, W. H., *Greek Passenger Liners* (Stroud, Gloucestershire, U.K.: Tempus, 2007); *Under the Red Ensign: British Passenger Liners of the '50s & '60s* (Stroud, Gloucestershire, U.K.: The History Press, 2009); *The Last Atlantic Liners* (London: Conway Maritime Press Ltd., 1985)

Newall, P., *Cunard Line: A Fleet History* (Longton, Preston, U.K.: Ships in Focus Publications, 2013); *Orient Line: A Fleet History* (Preston, Lancashire: Ships in Focus Publications, 2004)

Plowman, P., *Emigrant Ships to Luxury Liners* (Kensington, Australia: NDSW Press, 1992)

Official Steamship Guide (New York City: Transportation Guides Inc., 1953–63)

Ships & the Sea (Milwaukee, Wisconsion: Kalmbach Publishing Co., 1950–60)

TSS Stefan Batory: Polish Ocean Line 1968–1988